A Companion to Baugh &

History
of the
English Language

Third Edition

Thomas Cable
University of Texas at Austin

Prentice Hall, Upper Saddle River, New Jersey 07458

©2002 by PEARSON EDUCATION, INC.
Upper Saddle River, New Jersey 07458

ISBN 0-13-096771-8

Printed in the United States of America

Contents

Preface

In teaching the second edition of this *Companion* since 1993 I have noted various changes to make, as have helpful colleagues: places where the directions were not as clear as I had assumed, more errors than I would have wished, an occasional cramped format where more space was needed. The third edition makes dozens of corrections and adjustments throughout to remedy problems such as these. There is also a new exercise in Chapter 10 to go with the new section, "Gender Issues and Linguistic Change," in the fifth edition of Albert C. Baugh and Thomas Cable's *A History of the English Language* (Upper Saddle River, NJ, 2002). The exercises on African American Vernacular English in Chapter 11 have been thoroughly revised.

As in the second edition, the division into eleven chapters follows the format of the *History,* the length of the chapters varying considerably. For those chapters where extensive supplementary examples, additional explanation, and exercises are useful, as in Chapter 3, "Old English," the discussion and questions have been woven around selected phrases and sentences that appear in the language of that period.

The standard concordances, dictionaries, glossaries, readers, anthologies, editions, and atlases have been not only indispensable but a pleasure to use—works such as those by Campbell; Klaeber; Sweet (rev. Whitelock); Bright (rev. Cassidy and Ringler); Bessinger; Bosworth and Toller; Venezky and Healey; Mitchell; Kurath, Kuhn, Reidy, and Lewis; Mossé; Baugh; Bennett and Smithers; Tatlock and Kennedy; McIntosh, Samuels, and Benskin; Jespersen; Visser; Cassidy; and the editors of both the original edition (with supplements) and the second edition of the *Oxford English Dictionary.* Where the indebtedness amounts to more than a line or two at once I have made acknowledgments in the footnotes.

In the spirit of its parent text, the *Companion* pays attention to the linguistic effects of social, political, and literary events. The maps are designed to set the geographical contexts for these cultural influences during the Indo-European period, the Middle Ages, and the eras of the British Empire and of American ascendancy. The pre-chapter on "The Sounds of English" contains phonetic information and exercises that should be helpful in most of the chapters that follow. The "Questions for Review" that begin each chapter give an overview of the most important topics in each period and serve as a checklist of items that should be familiar in any discussion of the history of English. The headings for most sections are followed by a corresponding section number in the *History.* On many topics the amount of exposition preceding the exercises varies more or less inversely with the amount in the *History,* the idea being to have a full discussion of important topics without a duplication between the two books. A few sections in the *Companion* have no corresponding section in the *History.*

For extensive suggestions about ways to improve the *Companion,* I am especially indebted this time around to Traugott Lawler, who also gave good help on the main text. By mutual agreement and mutual preference, Carole Cable and I almost never read each other's proofs, but in the urgency of the present project she generously came to my aid, and I am grateful.

T.C.

Maps

0

The Sounds of English

0.1 PHONETICS SYMBOLS

Vowels

[ɑ]	father
[a]	French **la**
[ɒ]	hot (in England)
[æ]	mat
[ɛ]	met
[e]	mate
[ɪ]	sit
[i]	meat
[ɔ]	law
[o]	note
[ʊ]	book
[u]	boot
[ə]	above
[y]	French **tu**

Diphthongs[1]

[ɑɪ]	line
[ɑʊ]	house
[ɔɪ]	boy

Consonants

[p]	pack
[t]	top
[k]	kiss
[b]	base
[d]	duck
[g]	give
[f]	foot
[θ]	thin
[s]	soap
[š]	shoe Also [ʃ]
[x]	German **ich**
[h]	high
[v]	vote
[ð]	then
[z]	zoo
[ž]	azure Also [ʒ]
[č]	**ch**op Also [tʃ]
[ǰ]	juice Also [dʒ]
[m]	make
[n]	nail
[ŋ]	sing
[l]	lean
[r]	rip
[j]	you
[w]	win

[1]The tense vowels [e, i, o, u] in English are sometimes considered diphthongs because of the off-glide that automatically follows, for example, *so* [soʊ]. See §0.4.13.

0.2 THE VOCAL TRACT

The diagram below shows the vocal tract and some of the important points at which the stream of air from the lungs can be constricted to produce the sounds of language.

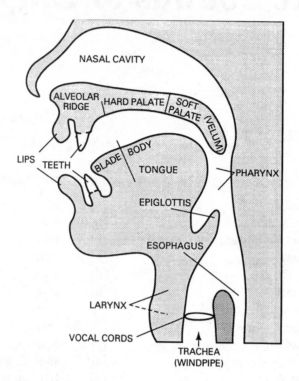

Figure 0.1

The following terms of articulatory phonetics refer to sounds produced at various points in the vocal tract. Identify the place where each sound is produced.

Velar	_____	Alveolar	_____
Palatal	_____	Labial	_____
Dental	_____	Labiodental	_____
Glottal	_____	Laryngeal	_____

0.3 ENGLISH CONSONANTS

The terms across the top of the chart refer to the *place* of articulation of English consonants; those on the left refer to the *manner* of articulation. Fill in the consonants of English in accordance with the discussion that follows.

The consonants are [b, č, d, f, g, h, j, ǰ, k, l, m, n, ŋ, p, r, s, š, t, θ, ð, v, w, z, ž].

	Bilabial	Labiodental	Dental	Alveolar	Palatal	Velar	Glottal
Stops							
Voiceless	[ ]			[ ]		[ ]	
Voiced	[ ]			[ ]		[ ]	
Fricatives							
Voiceless		[ ]	[ ]	[ ]	[ ]		[ ]
Voiced		[ ]	[ ]	[ ]	[ ]		
Affricates							
Voiceless					[ ]		
Voiced					[ ]		
Nasals	[ ]			[ ]		[ ]	
Liquids							
Lateral				[ ]			
Retroflex				[ ]			
Glides					[ ]	[ ]	

The initial sounds in *pin, tin,* and *kin* are alike in several features, but they are produced at different points in the vocal tract. The [p], made with both lips, is a **bilabial;** the [t], made by the tongue's striking the alveolar ridge, is an **aveolar;** and the [k], which requires the tongue to raise and retract, is made at the velum and is a **velar.** Enter these consonants on the first line of the chart (voiceless stops) in their appropriate brackets.

Stops, which are sometimes called **plosives,** are made with a sudden release of air. They contrast with **fricatives** (or **spirants**), which can be pronounced as continuous sounds until the speaker runs out of breath. Compare the initial stops in *pin, tin,* and *kin* with the initial fricatives in *fin* [f], *thin* [θ], *sin* [s]. *shin* [š], and *hen* [h]. Also, in pronouncing *fin, thin, sin, shin, hen,* notice that the tongue progressively retracts. The [f] in *fin,* made with the upper teeth and lower lip, is a **labiodental;** the [θ], made with the tongue between the teeth, is a **dental;** the [s] is an **aveolar;** the [š] a **palatal;**[2] and the [h] a **glottal.** Enter the symbols for these five consonants on the chart.

The [p] in *pat* and the [b] in *bat* are alike in being bilabial stops. The [p], however, is **voiceless** and the [b] is **voiced.** Voicing is produced by vibration of the vocal cords. Practice saying the two consonants until you hear the difference; then enter [b] in the appropriate brackets on the chart. The [d] in *do* and the [g] in *go* are also voiced stops, which correspond to the other two voiceless stops on the chart. Decide which is the alveolar sound and which is the velar, and fill in the appropriate symbols.

The four voiced fricatives are [v, ð, z, ž]. The [v] in *vat* and the [z] in *zip* are easily recognizable in comparison with the [f] in *fat* and the [s] in *sip,* respectively. The *th-* spelling is used for both the voiced dental fricative [ð] in *then* and the voiceless dental fricative [θ] in *thin. Thy* and *thigh* illustrate the same distinction. The voiced palatal fricative [ž] (see footnote 2) does not occur initially in English words but can be heard medially in words such as *measure* and *leisure.* Enter the symbols for the voiced fricatives on the chart.

The initial sounds in *chip* and *judge* are **affricates,** symbolized by [č] and [ǰ], respectively (see footnote 2). Affricates are consonants that begin as stops and become fricatives. The voiceless affricate can be considered a combination of [t] and [š] and the voiced affricate a combination of [d] and [ž]. Decide which is the voiced and which is the voiceless fricative and enter the symbols on the chart.

---

[2]An alternative symbol for [š] is [ʃ]. Systems of transcription that use this latter symbol usually also have [ʒ] for [ž], [tʃ] for [č] and [dʒ] for [ǰ].

Nasals should give little difficulty in identification and transcription. The three nasals occur at the bilabial, alveolar, and velar positions. Two of these are illustrated by the [n] in *need* and the [m] in *mead.* Decide which occurs where and enter the symbols on the chart. The third nasal is symbolized by a symbol that is not familiar from standard orthography, [ŋ], called *eng.* Pronounce the words *singer* and *finger,* both of which contain [ŋ]. For most speakers *finger* has the medial combination [ŋg], while *singer* has only [ŋ]. Practice pronouncing the sound and enter the symbol [ŋ] in the appropriate place on the chart.

The **liquids** in English consist of the **lateral** [l], so called because of the passage of air around the side of the tongue, and the **retroflex** [r]. Enter both of these in the alveolar position.

The **glides** (or **semivowels**) occur only before or after vowels and are vowel-like. The palatal [j] occurs at the beginning of *yes* and the labiovelar [w] at the beginning of *win.* Enter [j] and [w] on the chart. The [w], which is a back sound with rounded lips, can be entered at the velar position.

0.4 ENGLISH VOWELS

As with consonants, it is useful to keep in mind a cross section of the vocal tract while considering vowels. Because of the shape of the mouth, one can imagine a trapezoidal pattern of vowels superimposed on the vocal tract:

Figure 0.2

The nine divisions of the trapezoid enable us to locate vowels according to whether they are made at the front or the back of the mouth and whether they are high in the mouth or low. A vowel that is made approximately in the upper left corner of the trapezoid, for example, is called a **high front vowel.** Since more than one vowel can occur in a single division of the trapezoid, it will be necessary to consider other features by which vowels are distinguished, especially **tenseness** and **rounding.** In Old and Middle English, **length** is also important.

We can now enlarge the trapezoid and identify the individual vowels of Modern English. Fill in the trapezoid on the basis of the instructions and questions that follow.

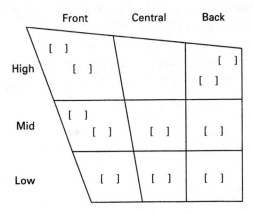

Figure 0.3

Place of Articulation

Three Maximum Contrasts

1. Say one after another the vowels in the words *beet, boot, father—ee, oo, ah*. The respective phonetic symbols for these vowels are [i, u, ɑ]. What happens to the tongue and chin in saying these sounds sequentially?_____

_____

2. For which of these sounds is the tongue lowest and the mouth most open?

_____

The sound is a low central vowel. Enter the appropriate symbol on the trapezoid above.

3. Now say one after another the remaining two sounds. For which of these sounds is the tongue further forward? _____ This sound is one of the two high front vowels in English. Enter the appropriate phonetic symbol on the trapezoid in the higher of the two available positions.

4. The remaining sound is a high back vowel. Write it on the trapezoid, also in the higher of the two positions.

These three sounds provide the maximum contrast of vowels in English. It is a pattern that occurs in many other languages as well.

Front Vowels

5. Say the vowels in the words *mat, mate, meet*. These are front vowels. We have already identified the last of these, the high front vowel [i]. The other two are the mid front vowel [e] (*mate*) and the low front vowel [æ] (*mat*). Write the appropriate symbols on the chart. Enter the mid front vowel in the higher of the two available positions.

Back Vowels

6. Say the vowels in the words *law, low, loose.* If your variety of English has the [ɑ]/[ɔ] contrast, the vowel in *law* is [ɔ]. The vowel in *low* is [o]. Enter these symbols on the trapezoid, [o] as a mid vowel, [ɔ] as a low vowel.

Note: In some varieties of American English the word *law* is pronounced with the same vowel as that of *father,* [ɑ]. Do you have the [ɑ]/[ɔ] contrast, or are words such as *cot* and *caught* pronounced the same? _____

Central Vowels

7. In addition to the low central [ɑ] of *father,* English has a very common central vowel that is made at the mid position of height, the [ə] which occurs in both syllables of *above.*[3] Write the symbol [ə] called *schwa,* in the appropriate place on the trapezoid.

Tense and Lax Vowels

8. Say the words *beet* and *bit.* The vowels of both of these words are made with the tongue high and forward in the mouth, and they are classed as high front vowels. They are commonly said to be distinguished as long and short vowels, a distinction that we shall see is historically important. But in present-day English, vowel length does not operate as it once did. The most important distinction now is between the tenseness and the laxness of the tongue, which may be difficult to detect. Lax vowels rarely occur at the end of a word; usually they are followed by a consonant. Tense vowels frequently end with a word and can occur in rhymes without a following consonant. Which word has a tense vowel, *beet* or *bit?* _____ The symbol for this vowel is already on the trapezoid. Enter the symbol [ɪ] for the vowel of *bit* in the remaining place in the high front position.

9. There is a similar distinction in tenseness between the vowels of *bait* and *bet.* Which of the two vowels is more tense (and occurs frequently at the end of a word)? _____ The symbol for this vowel is already on the trapezoid. Enter the symbol [ɛ] for the lax vowel of *bet* in the mid front position.

10. Say *pool* and *pull.* For which of these two words is the vowel already indicated on the trapezoid? _____
The symbol for the other vowel is [ʊ]. Enter it in the high back position on the trapezoid. Which is more tense, [u] or [ʊ]? _____

Round and Unround Vowels

11. Say the whole series of back vowels [ɔ, o, ʊ, u] and compare them with the front vowels [æ, ɛ, e, ɪ, i]. Aside from frontness and backness, what feature distinguishes the two

---

[3]In some systems of transcription, a distinction is made between the unstressed vowel, symbolized [ə], and the stressed vowel, symbolized [ʌ].

groups? Pay attention to the lips. _____

_____

12. Although you automatically rounded your lips for the back vowels and unrounded them for the front vowels, frontness does not coincide with unrounding and backness with rounding in every language. The vowel in French *une,* for example, is a high front rounded vowel, and when we study the older stages of English we will see that Old English had this sound too.

Diphthongs

13. A diphthong is a complex vowel sound in which two separate elements can be identified. In most dialects of present-day English, all the tense vowels can be considered diphthongs—at least phonetically. They consist of a nucleus and in varying degrees an off-glide. *Play,* for example, can be transcribed [pleɪ], the [ɪ] indicating a glide toward a high front sound. At a more abstract level than the narrowly phonetic, however, it is not necessary to transcribe the off-glide of *play,* because it occurs predictably and there is no significant contrast between [pleɪ] and [ple]. Therefore, in the broad transcription that we are doing, we will ignore the glides for all vowels except for three: those in *I* [ɑɪ], *out* [ɑʊ], and *joy* [ɔɪ]. The glides in these vowels are necessary to distinguish such words as *joy* [jŏɪ] and *jaw* [jŏ].

14. The chart below shows the diphthongs [ɑɪ], [ɑʊ], and [ɔɪ]. These may or may not be accurate for your own dialect. Many speakers in the South and Southwest, for example, have [a:] instead of [ɑɪ] in the pronoun *I,* while speakers in Virginia may have [əɪ] in *I* and [əʊ] in *out.* In Chaps. 10 and 11 we will consider present-day variations of these sounds.

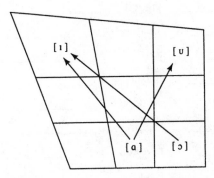

Figure 0.4

15. Pronounce the word *I* with exaggerated slowness, prolonging the syllable for several seconds. Are there two sounds in your pronunciation? _____

16. Pronounce *out* with the same prolongation. What sound occurs? _____

17. Pronounce *boy* very slowly. What sounds occur? _____

0.5 TRANSCRIPTION

Use the phonetic notation from the preceding sections to transcribe the following words.

map	straw	blue
seek	shop	crime
dim	those	mouse
paste	thin	mice
head	reach	breath
would	yell	breathe
choose	gauge	spoil
luck	joke	known
frown	view	word
tricked	brief	term
matched	ought	thing
blamed	bird	think
sneezed	burglar	distinct
joined	watching	throbbing
rounded	loaded	useful
pickle	rated	music
amaze	jagged	lawyer
release	shadow	needle
balloon	partial	weather
exert	massive	gaslight
poaching	wooded	wildcat
treasure	rapture	fishbowl
smoothest	revoked	earthquake
situation	icicle	antelope
historian	truism	strategy
diaphragm	equity	zucchini
sovereign	tuxedo	socialist
judicial	natural	chivalry
furious	rebellion	dangerous
powerful	nuclear	authentic
opinion	horrify	marathon
excessive	avenue	miniscule

1

English Present and Future

1.1 QUESTIONS FOR REVIEW

1. Define the following terms, which appear in Chapter 1 of Baugh and Cable, *A History of the English Language* (5th ed.):

Analogy
Borrowing
Inflection
Natural gender
Grammatical gender
Idiom
Lingua franca

2. Upon what does the importance of a language depend?

3. About how many people speak English as a native language?

4. Which language of the world has the largest number of speakers?

5. What are the six largest European languages after English?

6. Why is English so widely used as a second language?

7. Which languages are likely to grow most rapidly in the foreseeable future? Why?

8. What are the official languages of the United Nations?

9. For a speaker of another language learning English, what are three assets of the language?

10. What difficulties does the non-native speaker of English encounter?

2

The Indo-European Family of Languages

2.1 QUESTIONS FOR REVIEW

1. Explain why the following people are important in studies of the Indo-European family of languages:

Panini
Ulfilas
Jacob Grimm
Karl Verner
Ferdinand de Saussure

2. Define, identify, or explain briefly:

Family of languages
Indo-European
Rig-veda
Koiné
Langue d'oïl, langue d'oc
Vulgar Latin
Proto-Germanic
Second Sound Shift
West Germanic
Hittites
Laryngeals
Object-Verb structure
Centum and *satem* languages
Kurgans

3. What is Sanskrit? Why is it important in the reconstruction of Indo-European?

4. When did the sound change described by Grimm's Law occur? In what year did Grimm formulate the law?

5. Name the eleven principal groups in the Indo-European family.

6. Approximately what date can be assigned to the oldest texts of Vedic Sanskrit?

7. From what non-Indo-European language has modern Persian borrowed much vocabulary?

8. Which of the dialects of ancient Greece was the most important? In what centuries did its literature flourish?

9. Why are the Romance languages so called? Name the modern Romance languages.

10. What were the important dialects of French in the Middle Ages? Which became the basis for standard French?

11. For the student of Indo-European, what is especially interesting about Lithuanian?

12. Name the Slavic languages. With what other group does Slavic form a branch of the Indo-European tree?

13. Into what three groups is the Germanic branch divided? For which of the Germanic languages do we have the earliest texts?

14. From what period do our texts of Scandinavian languages date?

15. Why is Old English classified as a Low German language?

16. Name the two branches of the Celtic family and the modern representative of each.

17. Where are the Celtic languages now spoken? What is happening to these languages?

18. What two languages of importance to Indo-European studies were discovered in this century?

19. Why have the words for *beech* and *bee* in the various Indo-European languages been important in establishing the location of the Indo-European homeland?

20. What light have recent archaeological discoveries thrown on the Indo-European homeland?

2.2 GRIMM'S LAW (§16)[1]

The chart on page 13 shows the traditional reconstruction of the Indo-European consonants that were affected by the sound changes known as Grimm's Law. During the past two decades, controversial new theories have proposed a different set of consonants in Indo-European and consequently a different development of the consonants in Germanic; these new, interrelated theories also require developments different from those traditionally assumed for the consonants in the non-Germanic languages.[2] However, the glottalic hypothesis at the center of these theories has problems of its own, and, unlike another famous reconstruction of the past century, Saussure's laryngeal theory, it has not yet been shown to have widespread application beyond the specific problem that it was designed to solve. We shall stay with the traditional account of Grimm's Law, which is probably the best-known of all sound laws and which at its formulation by Rasmus Rask in 1818 and by Jacob Grimm in 1822 became the cornerstone of historical and comparative linguistics in the nineteenth century.

---

[1]Numbers in parentheses refer to corresponding sections in *A History of the English Language*.

[2]Briefly, the voiced stops are reconstructed as voiceless ejective, or glottalized, stops, and each of the consonants in the other two series is reconstructed as a pair of allophones. One advantage of this system is that the puzzling series of voiced aspirates /bh dh gh/, for which no one knows the Indo-European pronunciation, are admitted to be strange; their very strangeness, in fact, was one of the reasons for proposing the new theory. See Paul J. Hopper, "'Decem' and 'Taihun' Languages: An Indo-European Isogloss," and Thomas V. Gamkrelidze, "Language Typology and Language Universals and Their Implications for the Reconstruction of the Indo-European Stop System," both in *Bono Homini Donum: Essays in Historical Linguistics, in Memory of J. Alexander Kerns*, ed. Y. L. Arbeitman and A. R. Bomhard (2 vols., Amsterdam: Benjamins, 1981), pp. 133–42, 571–609. See also Andrew Garrett, "Indo-European Reconstruction and Historical Methodologies," *Language*, 67 (1991), 790–804.

Indo-European Consonants					
	Bilabial	Labiodental	Dental	Alveolar	Palatal	Velar
Stops						
Voiceless	p			t		k
Voiced	b			d		g
Aspirates						
Voiced	bh			dh		gh

Summary of Grimm's Law[3]

bh → β → b   dh → ð → d   gh → γ → g
p → f   t → θ   k → x
b → p   d → t   g → k

These shifts are assumed to have occurred in a certain sequence:

(1) bh, dh, gh   → β, ð, γ
(2) p, t, k   → f, θ x
(3) b, d, g   → p, t, k
(4) β, ð, γ   → b, d, g

1. The following four charts show the configuration of the Proto-Germanic consonants after each stage of the consonant shift. Fill in the three solid lines on each chart with the appropriate symbols for the new sounds. (The dotted lines represent the sound of the previous stage. Leave them blank.)

Proto-Germanic after (1)					
	Bilabial	Labiodental	Dental	Alveolar	Palatal	Velar
Stops						
Voiceless	p			t		k
Voiced	b			d		g
Fricatives						
Voiced	___		___			___
Aspirates						
Voiced	…			…		…

[3]The symbol /β/ represents a voiced bilabial fricative; /γ/ and /x/ are the velar fricatives, voiced and voiceless, respectively. Slanted brackets are used in this exercise to indicate broad, or phonemic, transcription, instead of the square brackets of phonetic transcription. This notation acknowledges that we do not know the phonetic values of /bh, dh, gh/ and that the whole set of reconstructed Indo-European consonants shows systematic phonological contrasts rather than narrow phonetic reality.

Proto-Germanic after (2)					
Bilabial	Labiodental	Dental	Alveolar	Palatal	Velar
Stops					
Voiceless ...			...		...
Voiced b			d		g
Fricatives					
Voiceless	—	—			—
Voiced β		ð			γ

Proto-Germanic after (3)					
Bilabial	Labiodental	Dental	Alveolar	Palatal	Velar
Stops					
Voiceless —			—		—
Voiced ...			...		...
Fricatives					
Voiceless	f	θ			x
Voiced β		ð			γ

Proto-Germanic after (4)					
Bilabial	Labiodental	Dental	Alveolar	Palatal	Velar
Stops					
Voiceless p			t		k
Voiced —			—		—
Fricatives					
Voiceless	f	θ			x
Voiced ...		...			...

2. Name the categories involved in the four changes.

(1) _____voiced aspirates_____ → _____voiced fricatives_____

(2) _____ → _____

(3) _____ → _____

(4) _____ → _____

3. For each of the reconstructed Indo-European roots listed below, complete the reconstructed Germanic derivative and the Old and Modern English words by supplying the consonant that resulted from the operation of Grimm's Law. (The same consonant occurs in Germanic, Old English, and Modern English.) For Indo-European voiced aspirates, give the final result, the voiced stops. For the sound [θ], write *th;* for [x] write *h*. For Old and Modern English [k] the spelling is often *c*. When two Indo-European roots are given, the first is the basic uninflected form and the second is the form to which the English word is more closely related.[4] To complete the last column, see exercise 4 below.

Indo-European[5]	Germanic	Old English	Modern English	Borrowing from Latin
*pisk-	*__iska-	__isc	__ish	_____
*ter-, *ter-sk- 'to rub, thresh'	*__ersk-	__erscan	__resh	_____
*kerd-, *kerd-en-	*__ertōn	__eorte	__eart	_____
*beu- 'to swell'	*__uk-	__yffan	__uff	_____
*dent-, *dont-	*__anthus	__ōþ	__ooth	_____
*gel- 'cold; to freeze'	*__ōl-	__ōl	__ool	_____
*bhreg-	*__rekan	__recan	__reak	_____
*dhē, *dhō- 'to set, put'	*__ōn	__ōn	__o	_____
*ghos-ti-	*__astiz	__estr[6]	__uest	_____
*ters-, *tr̥s-t- 'to dry'	*__urs-tu-	__urst	__irst	_____
*dhwer-, *dhur-	*__uram	__or	__oor	_____
*ker-, *kr̥-n-	*__urnaz	__orn	__orn	_____
*grə-no- 'grain'	*__ornam	__orn	__orn	_____
*kaput	*__aubidam	__ēafod	__ead	_____
*bher- 'to carry; to bear children'	*__eran	__eran	__ear	_____
*pleus- 'to pluck; feather, fleece'	*__liusaz	__lēos	__leece	_____
*bhedh- 'to dig'	*__adjam 'garden plot'	__edd	__ed	_____
*dekm̥	*__ehun	__īen	__en	_____
*ger- 'to cry hoarsely'	*__rē	__rāwe	__row	_____
*trei-	*__rijiz	__rīe	__ree	_____

[4]The source for the items in this exercise is the appendix entitled "Indo-European Roots" of *The American Heritage Dictionary of the English Language,* 4th ed. (New York: American Heritage Publishing Co. and Houghton Mifflin, 2000).

[5]The Indo-European roots given here without a gloss have at least one meaning the same as that of the Modern English form.

[6]This word is not a native Old English word but an Old Norse borrowing in Middle English.

Indo-European	Germanic	Old English	Modern English	Borrowing from Latin
*genə, *gn̥-yo- 'to give birth'	*__unjam 'family'	__ynn	__in	_____
*deik-, *deig- 'to show, pronounce'	*__aikjan	__ǣċan	__each	_____
*kel-, *kl̥-ni-	*__ulni-	__yll	__ill	_____
*teuə-, *tum- 'to swell'	*__ūmōn	__ūma 'thick finger'	__umb	_____
*pau-	*__awaz	__ēawe	__ew	_____
*bhlē-	*__lē-w	__lāwan	__low	_____
*ten-, *tn̥-u- 'stretched, thin'	*__unniz	__ynne	__in	_____
*ped-, *pōd	*__ōt-	__ōt	__oot	_____
*genu-, *gneu-	*__niwam	__nēo	__nee	_____

4. Although the Germanic part of what eventually became the English vocabulary underwent the First Sound Shift, thousands of words have entered the English language in the centuries afterwards. Borrowings from Latin illustrate clearly the effects of Grimm's Law by the changes that did *not* happen to them. Many of the Latin borrowings retain the original Indo-European consonants: [p], [t], and [k], for example, remained [p], [t], and [k] in Latin ([k] being spelled *c*), and [b], [d], and [g] remained [b], [d], and [g]. Indo-European [bh] and [dh] became Latin [f], and [gh] became [h]. The Latin words listed below are given with a gloss and, in boldface type, an English borrowing based on the Latin, either directly or through Romance languages. Match the borrowed words with the English words that derive ultimately from the same Indo-European root by writing the boldfaced Modern English borrowings in the last column of question 3, above.

dēns 'tooth': **dental**
caput 'head': **capital**
piscis 'fish': **Pisces**
facere 'to do, make': **fashion**
glaciēs 'ice': **glacial**
torrēre 'to dry, parch, burn': **torrid**
bucca '(inflated) cheek': **buccal**
frangere 'to break': **fracture**
pēs (stem *ped-*) 'foot': **pedal**
culmen 'top, summit': **culminate**
grāculus 'jackdaw': **grackle**
forās 'out of doors': **foreign**
tendere 'to stretch, extend': **extend**
plūma 'a feather': **plume**

grānum: **grain**
paucus 'little, few': **paucity**
dīcere 'to say, tell': **dictate**
cor 'heart': **cordial**
fodere 'to dig': **fossil**
trēs 'three': **trio**
genu 'knee': **genuflect**
terere 'to rub away, wear out': **trite**
decem 'ten': **decimal**
flare 'to blow': **inflate**
tumēre 'to swell': **tumescent**
cornū 'horn': **cornet**
genus 'race, kind': **genus**
ferre 'to carry': **fertile**
hostis 'enemy': **host**

2.3 THE INDO-EUROPEAN FAMILY (§§17–27)

Complete the Indo-European family tree on page 18 by filling in the names of the missing languages: Albanian, Armenian, Breton, Bulgarian, Czech, Danish, Dutch, English, French, Greek, High German, Icelandic, Irish, Italian, Latvian, Lithuanian, Norwegian, Persian, Polish, Portuguese, Romanian, Russian, Scottish Gaelic, Spanish, Swedish, and Welsh. The numbers refer to countries on the map of present-day Europe (p. 20) where the languages are spoken. The former Yugoslavia consists of the republics (from north to south) of Slovenia, Croatia, Bosnia and Herzegovina, Yugoslavia (including Serbia and Montenegro), and the Former Yugoslav Republic of Macedonia.

2.4 THE INDO-EUROPEANS (§28)

The map on p. 19 shows possible paths of Proto-Indo-European expansion as inferred from recent archaeological discoveries.[7] Each wave brought about a transformation of the culture that had preceded it. Wave #1 resulted in an amalgamation of the warlike Proto-Indo-Europeans and the sedentary, peaceful people of Old Europe, whose economy was purely agricultural. Wave #2, which was probably the most important for the formation of Indo-Europeanized Europe and Anatolia, completed the transformation of the social structure from a society that was matricentric and egalitarian to one that was patriarchal and sharply classed. There were changes also in the patterns of habitation and architecture, in the intensification of the pastoral economy, in metallurgical technology, and in cult and religion.

Turn the information on the map into a one-paragraph narrative on the spread of the Indo-European (or Kurgan) culture. Where was the Indo-European homeland, according to the theory on which this map is based? What area was subjected to three waves of Indo-Europeans during the course of two millennia? When did the Indo-Europeans spread to the British Isles? What parts of Europe had not been infiltrated by the Indo-Europeans as late as 2300 B.C.? Use the map of modern Europe on p. 20 to refer to areas by their present-day names.

[7]Adapted by permission of the *Journal of Indo-European Studies* and with the help of Marija Gimbutas from her series of studies, especially "The First Wave of Eurasian Steppe Pastoralists into Copper Age Europe," *JIES,* 5 (1977), 312, 331, and "The Kurgan Wave #2 (*c.* 3400–3200 B.C.) into Europe and the Following Transformation of Culture," *JIES,* 8 (1980), 275.

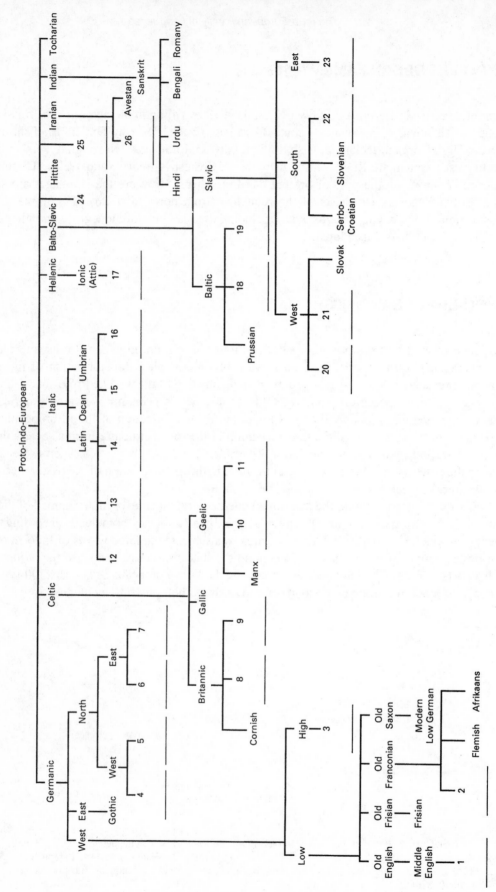

Figure 2.1

18

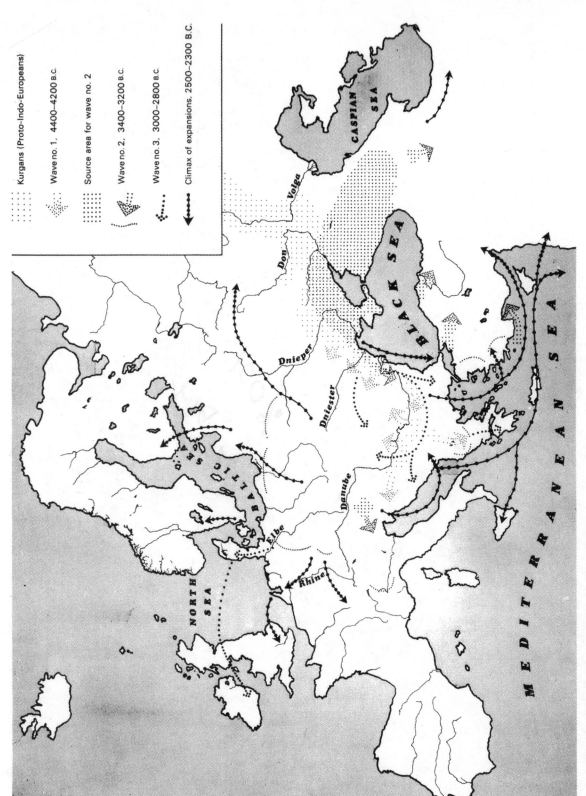

Figure 2.2 The Expansion of the Indo-Europeans.

Kurgans (Proto-Indo-Europeans)

Wave no. 1. 4400–4200 B.C.

Source area for wave no. 2

Wave no. 2. 3400–3200 B.C.

Wave no. 3. 3000–2800 B.C.

Climax of expansions. 2500–2300 B.C.

CASPIAN SEA

Volga

Don

BLACK SEA

Dnieper

Dniester

Danube

Elbe

Rhine

BALTIC SEA

NORTH SEA

MEDITERRANEAN SEA

19

20

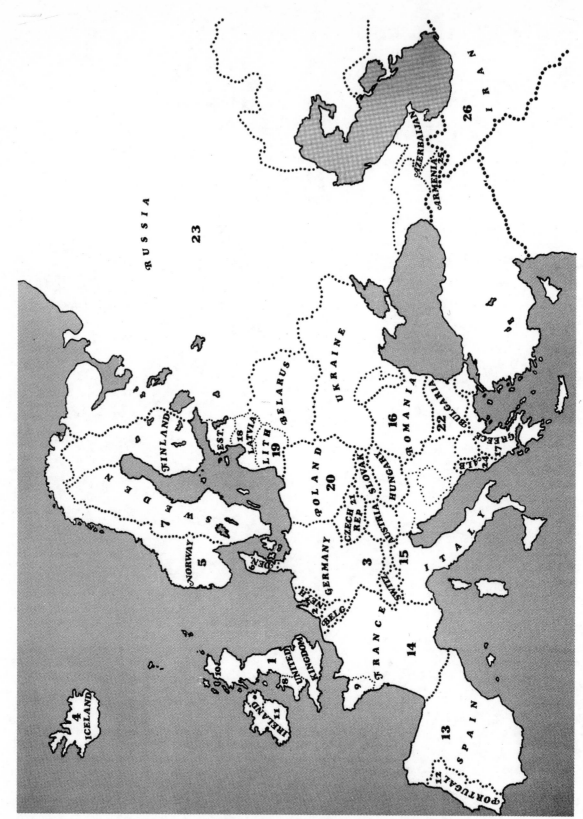

Figure 2.3   Present-Day Europe.

3

Old English

3.1 QUESTIONS FOR REVIEW

1. Explain why the following are important in historical discussions of the English language:

Claudius
Vortigern
The Anglo-Saxon Heptarchy
Beowulf
Alfred the Great
Ecclesiastical History of the English People

2. Define the following terms:

Synthetic language
Analytic language
Vowel declension
Consonant declension
Grammatical gender
Dual number
Paleolithic Age
Neolithic Age

3. Who were the first people in England about whose language we have definite knowledge?

4. When did the Romans conquer England, and when did they withdraw?

5. At approximately what date did the invasion of England by the Germanic tribes begin?

6. Where were the homes of the Angles, Saxons, and Jutes?

7. Where does the name *English* come from?

8. What characteristics does English share with other Germanic languages?

9. To which branch of Germanic does English belong?

10. What are the dates of Old English, Middle English, and Modern English?

11. What are the four dialects of Old English?

12. About what percentage of the Old English vocabulary is no longer in use?

13. Explain the difference between *strong* and *weak* declensions of adjectives.

14. How does the Old English definite article differ from the definite article of Modern English?

15. Explain the difference between *weak* and *strong* verbs.

16. How many classes of strong verbs were there in Old English?

17. In what ways was the Old English vocabulary expanded?

3.2 OLD ENGLISH CONSONANTS (§40)

In the Old English writing system the letters *b, d, l, m, p, t,* and *w* represented the same sounds as in Modern English. The *r* was probably trilled.

The combinations *sc* and *cg* represented the sounds [š] and [ǰ], respectively, as in *disc* [dɪš] 'dish' and *hrycg* [hryǰ] 'ridge'.

The rest of the symbols that represented consonants in the Old English writing system, *f, þ, ð, s, n, h, c,* and *g,* did double duty, each standing for two distinct sounds. The sound that occurred in any specific context can readily be determined from phonological regularities that the sounds reflect.

```
OE SPELLING            f           þ, ð            s
                      / \         /  \           / \
                     /   \       /    \         /   \
SOUND              [f]   [v]   [θ]    [ð]     [s]   [z]
```

F, þ, ð, and *s* represented both voiced and voiceless sounds in Old English. They are grouped together here because the contexts for voicing or unvoicing were the same for all three fricatives. The letters þ (thorn) and ð (eth) were used more or less interchangeably by Old English scribes.

The **voiced fricatives** [v, ð, z] occurred only between voiced sounds within words, as in *hlāford* [hlɑ:vɔrd] 'lord'.

Elsewhere the **voiceless fricatives** [f, θ, s] occurred, as in the following contexts:

a. At the beginning of a word: *flōd* [flo:d] 'flood'
b. At the end of a word: *lēaf* [læ:əf] 'leaf'
c. Next to a voiceless sound: *sceaft* [šæəft] 'shaft'
d. Doubled: *pyffan* [pyffɑn] 'to puff'

```
OE SPELLING                        n
                                  / \
                                 /   \
SOUND                          [n]   [ŋ]
```

The letter *n* was pronounced [n] except before [g] or [k] (spelled *c,* occasionally *k*). In these combinations it was pronounced [ŋ], and the following [g] or [k] was also pronounced, as in Modern English *finger: singan* [sɪŋgɑn] 'to sing'.

OE SPELLING

SOUND   [h]   [x]

The letter *h* at the beginning of words was pronounced with a light aspiration, like the Modern English glottal fricative [h]: *ham* [hɑ:m] 'home'. Elsewhere it was pronounced with stronger aspiration, like the fricatives in German *ich, Bach* and Scots *loch* 'lake' [x]: *seah* [sæəx] 'saw'.[1] The [h] could be followed by a liquid to form consonant clusters, which have since been simplified: *hlāf* [hlɑ:f] 'loaf', *hring* [hrɪŋg] 'ring'.

OE SPELLING   c   g

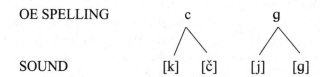

SOUND   [k]   [č]   [j]   [g]

The letter *c* represented Old English [k] and [č]; the letter *g* represented [j] and [g].[2] Since the determining context is sometimes a sound that occurred at an earlier stage of the language but did not occur at the date of our texts, we will use a modern editorial device, a dot above the letter, for indicating the palatalized sounds: *ċ* [č] as in *ċēosan* [če:ozɑn] 'to choose'; *ġ* [j] as in *ġēar* [jæ:ər] 'year', *dysiġ* [dyzɪj] 'foolish' (cf. Modern English *dizzy*). Examples of the velar consonants are *clǣne* [klæ:nɛ] 'clean' and *gōd* [go:d] 'good'.

1. Write each of the Old English words from the list below in an appropriate blank to show whether the italicized fricative is voiced or voiceless. Bear in mind two points: (1) the voiced fricatives [v, ð, z] occur between voiced sounds, and the voiceless fricatives [f, θ, s] occur elsewhere; (2) *voiced sounds* include all liquids and nasals as well as all vowels and voiced stops and fricatives.

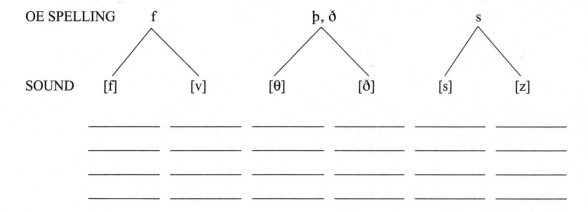

OE SPELLING   f   þ, ð   s

SOUND   [f]   [v]   [θ]   [ð]   [s]   [z]

---

[1]An *h* after a vowel is palatal, while an *h* after a back vowel is velar. Although different phonetic symbols could be used to show this difference (for example, [ç] for the *h* in *niht* 'night' and [x] for the *h* in *noht* 'not'), in Old English the difference is allophonic—that is, the adjustments in fronting are made automatically, and a single symbol [x] suffices.

[2]In addition to [j] and [g], *g* represented the voiced velar fricative, symbolized by [ɣ]. See Richard M. Hogg, *A Grammar of Old English, Volume 1: Phonology* (Oxford: Blackwell, 1992), §7.2. It will suffice for our purposes to pronounce the two velar variants of *g* as [g].

sǣ 'sea'   lyƒt 'air'
brōðor 'brother'   yrhðo 'slackness'
wīƒ 'woman'   oƒfrian 'to offer'
hræƒn 'raven'   bōsm 'bosom'
missenlīċ 'various'   oððe 'or'
ƒlota 'ship'   wæs 'was'
ċeaster 'city'   þeġn 'thane'
lēoð 'song'   eƒne 'even'
weorþe 'worthy'   nosu 'nose'
oƒer 'over'   blīþe 'joyous'
rīsan 'to rise'   heoƒon 'heaven'
æþele 'noble'   hæslen 'of hazel'

2. Part of the initial strangeness of a page of Old English is due simply to the differences in conventions of spelling between the older period and the present one. With an understanding of the scribal practices for consonants sketched above, we can see that the pronunciation of a large number of Old English words is close to that of their Modern English descendants—and sometimes exactly the same. In the following list of words the phonetic symbols of the Old English vowels are provided. Supply the phonetic symbols for the consonants, say the words aloud, and deduce the Modern English forms.

OE Spelling	OE Pronunciation	Modern Spelling
bæð	[__ æ __]	_____
æfter	[æ __ ɛ __]	_____
scip	[__ ɪ __]	_____
ecg	[ɛ __]	_____
drifen	[__ ɪ __ ɛ __]	_____
biter	[__ ɪ __ ɛ __]	_____
weġ	[__ ɛ __]	_____
stenċ	[__ ɛ __]	_____
ofer	[ɔ __ ɛ __]	_____
bliss	[__ ɪ __]	_____
feðer	[__ ɛ __ ɛ __]	_____
fisc	[__ ɪ __]	_____
blæc	[__ æ __]	_____
scield	[__ ɪə __]	_____
seġl	[__ ɛ __]	_____
fæst	[__ æ __]	_____
wið	[__ ɪ __]	_____
bæc	[__ æ __]	_____
hwæþer	[__ æ __ ɛ __]	_____

OE Spelling	OE Pronunciation	Modern Spelling
hefiġ	[__ ɛ __ ɪ __]	_____
norð	[__ ɔ __]	_____
leġd	[__ ɛ __]	_____
arċebiscop	[ɑ __ ɛ __ ɪ __ ɔ __]	_____
goldfinċ³	[__ ɔ __ ɪ __]	_____
æsc-grǣġ	[æ __ æ: __]	_____

3.3 OLD ENGLISH VOWELS (§40)

In the preceding exercise the similarities between the sounds of Old English and those of Modern English are found in the consonants and the short vowels. The long vowels of Middle English changed radically but systematically during the fifteenth century (as we will see in Chap. 8). Before this shift, the long vowels of the English language were closer in quality to the vowels of other European languages, and, as shown below, the orthographic symbols for those vowels correspond closely to the modern phonetic symbols that we studied in Chapter 1.

Spelling	Sound	Example
a	[ɑ]	camp [kɑmp] 'battle'
ā	[ɑ:]	hlāf [hlɑ:f] 'loaf'
æ	[æ]	æt [æt] 'at'
ǣ	[æ:]	lǣst [læ:st] 'least'
e	[ɛ]	wel [wɛl] 'well'
ē	[e:]	cwēn [kwe:n] 'queen'
i	[ɪ]	hit [hɪt] 'it'
ī	[i:]	wīs [wi:s] 'wise'
o	[ɔ]	folc [fɔlk] 'people'
ō	[o:]	sōð [so:θ] 'truth'
u	[ʊ]	hund [hʊnd] 'dog'
ū	[u:]	nū [nu:] 'now'
y	[y]	wyrm [wyrm] 'serpent'
ȳ	[y:]	hȳd [hy:d] 'hide'
ea	[æə]	heall [hæəl] 'hall'
ēa	[æ:ə]	dēad [dæ:əd] 'dead'
eo	[ɛo]	deorc [dɛork] 'dark'
ēo	[e:o]	frēond [fre:ond] 'friend'

While most of the sounds and symbols that you will encounter in Old English will be familiar from Modern English transcriptions, three features may seem strange—vocalic length, rounding of the high front vowel, and diphthongs.

Vocalic Length.   A **long vowel** in Old English is actually prolonged in time. This contrasts with Modern English, where the common use of "long" and "short" refers to features that may more accurately be described as "tense" and "lax." The temporal distinction between long and short vowels was important in Old English meter, and it was more basic in the language

---

³The rules of voicing do not apply between the elements of a compound word. To determine the sound of *f,* consider *gold* and *finċ* as two separate words.

generally than the secondary distinction based on quality.[4] Say *æt* 'at' and *ǣt* 'ate' so that length distinguishes the two words. We'll transcribe long vowels with a colon: *ǣt* [æ:t]

Rounding.   The high front vowel [y] occurs in French *une* but not in Modern English. Say the [i] sound of *marine* and round the lips, taking care that the vowel remains front and does not become the [u] of *maroon*. The long vowel [y:] is the same sound prolonged.

Diphthongs.   The diphthongs contain familiar elements combined in unfamiliar ways. Take care to pronounce them as falling diphthongs, with more stress on the first element than on the second.

Fill in the charts below to show the vowels and diphthongs of Old English. For pairs of long and short vowels, enter the long vowel in the higher space provided.

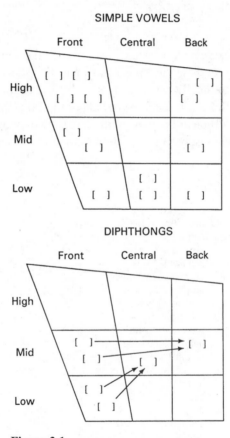

Figure 3.1

3.4 OLD ENGLISH SUPRASEGMENTALS

The stress pattern of Old English is easy to learn because it follows the Germanic pattern of primary stress on the first syllable of the word. Secondary, tertiary, and weak stresses almost take care of themselves when one understands that the prevailing stress contour of Old English

---

[4]It is impossible to know the exact quality of the vowels of Old English. We will assume that the long and short varieties of the other pairs of vowels were qualitatively different. See Hogg *op. cit.,* §2.8. But cf. A. Campbell, *Old English Grammar* (Oxford: Oxford University Press, 1959), §31*n*2, who describes *all* pairs of long and short vowels before 1200 as differing in length alone, all being tense, the laxing of short vowels coming about as a later development.

is a descending contour. (This contrasts with the prevailing pattern of alternating stress in Modern English, a result of the high proportion of Romance vocabulary.) For word stress, two rules are useful:

Rule 1. The heaviest stress of a word occurs on the first syllable, except for verbal prefixes (*ġe-, be-, ā-, on-, wið-, for-, under-, ofer-, ymb-,* etc.).

       /   x   /   x   x   /   x

Examples: dohtor 'daughter', hlude 'loudly', be-settan 'surround'

Rule 2. Secondary stress occurs on the second element of compounds.

       /   \   /   x   \   /   \ x

Examples: eorð-weġ 'earthly way', ıren-heard 'iron-hard', fea-lufu 'love of money'

In phrases and sentences, nouns and adjectives are more heavily stressed than verbs and adverbs, which in turn are more heavily stressed than pronouns, articles, prepositions, and conjunctions. The stress on verbs and adverbs varies in strength, depending on their position in the sentence.

1. Mark the pattern of stress in the following words, using / for main stress, \ for secondary stress, and *x* for weak stress. Prefixes and elements of compound words are set apart by hyphens. Remember that prefixes of *verbs* are weakly stressed; *nouns* and *adjectives* with prefixes are stressed like compounds, with full stress on the prefix and secondary stress on the second element. The first word has been marked as an example.

    /   x   \

wundor-deað 'wondrous death'	on-findan 'to discover'
land 'land'	on-weald 'dominion'
healdan 'to hold'	for-grindan 'to grind to pieces'
wæter 'water'	for-heard 'very hard'
brōðer 'brother'	ðurh-crēopan 'to creep through'
be-cuman 'to come'	ðurh-hefiġ 'very heavy'
wið-standan 'to withstand'	ymb-gān 'to go round'
ā-hebban 'to lift up'	ymb-hwyrft 'rotation'
ġe-drincan 'to drink up'	līf-dagas 'life-days'
sǣ-strand 'sea shore'	swan-rād 'swan-road', 'sea'
hring-net 'coat of mail'	lēod-sceaða 'people's enemy'
hord-burh 'treasure-city'	gūð-weriġ 'weary with fighting'
wīd-cūþ 'widely known'	leorning-cniht 'disciple'

2. The meter of Old English poetry was based on stress patterns such as the ones that you have marked above. There is evidence that these patterns were crystallized and made distinct by the suprasegmental feature of **pitch.** For Old English poetry, one can postulate melodic contours, or tunes, to which the epics were sung. Opposite are the opening lines of *Beowulf,* marked with both the linguistic stresses and the inferred contours of melody.[5]

---

[5]See Thomas Cable, *The Meter and Melody of Beowulf* (Urbana: University of Illinois Press, 1974), pp. 94–110.

Figure 3.2

3.5 OLD ENGLISH CASES (§40)

Grammatical function—subject, object, etc.—is indicated by case endings. (It is the subsequent loss of these endings that causes Modern English to rely more basically on word order in signaling function.) The main functions of the five cases of Old English nouns and pronouns are as listed below.

Nominative

Subject: Sēo *stōw* is ġehāten 'Heofonfeld' on Englisc.
      That place is called   'Heavenfield'   in   English.

Subject complement: Bēowulf is mīn *nama*.

Beowulf   is my   name.

Direct address: *Cedmon,* sing mē hwæthwugu.

Cædmon,   sing me something.

Accusative

Direct object: Hē þone *fēond* ofercwōm.

He that   enemy   overcame.

Adverbial noun of time: Wunodon þǣr ealne þone *winter*.

(They) stayed there all   that   winter.

Note: See also *Instrumental.*

Object of prepositions implying movement: Ġewāt þā ofer *wǣgholm*.

(It) went then over sea.

Note: Prepositions implying movement sometimes take the dative, and the accusative is sometimes used when no movement is implied.

Genitive

Possession: *Godes* mildheortnys ūs forestæpð.

God's   mercy   us precedes.

Genitive of measure:

þǣr wearþ Cīrus ofslæġen ond twā þūsend monna mid him.

There was   Cyrus   slain   and two thousand men   with him.

Object of verbs of depriving: Cynewulf benam Siġebryht his *rīċes*.

Cynewulf   deprived Sigebryht of his kingdom.

Dative

Object of most prepositions: Crīst wæs on *rōde*.

Christ was on cross.

Indirect object: Sē kyng þā ġeaf gryð *Ōlāfe*.

That king then gave truce Olaf.

Sole object of certain verbs: Hyra *fēore* burgon.

Their life (they) saved.

Expression of means or manner without a preposition:

Ic him þēnode dēoran sweorde.

I   them served   (with) excellent sword.

Instrumental

Note: The instrumental has merged with the dative and occurs only occasionally in Old English. There are separate forms for the masculine and neuter definite article but no separate forms for the noun.

Object of prepositions expressing means or manner:

þā scēat hē mid þȳ *spere.*

Then thrust he with that spear.

Object of prepositions expressing accompaniment:

Oferfōr hē mid þȳ *folce.*

Traversed he with that people.

Adverbial noun of time: Ond þȳ ilcan *ġeare* fōr sē here ofer sǽ.

And that same   year   went that army over sea.

The passage below is a fairly literal translation from the *Anglo-Saxon Chronicle,* about half the entry for the year 894. The Old English noun phrases and pronouns that appear in parentheses in the Modern English translation are listed below the text with their cases. Explain the choice of case for each by naming the function of the noun or pronoun in the sentence.

894. And then immediately after that, in this year, *the Viking army (sē here)*[1] marched from Wirral in on the Welsh, because they were not able to stay there: that was because they were deprived of [*benumene,* past participle of *beniman* 'to deprive of'] both *the cattle (þæs ċeapes)*[2] and *the grain (þæs cornes)*[3] that they [the English] had captured. When *they (hīe)*[4] turned back out from the Welsh with *the plunder (þǽre herehȳðe)*[5] which they had seized there, they then marched over the *Northumbrians' (Norðhymbra)*[6] *land (lond)*[7] and also the East Anglians', so that *the [English] army (sēo fird)*[8] could not reach *them (hīe)*[9]—until they came on the eastern part of the East Saxons' land onto *an island (an īġland)*[10] that is out on *the sea (þǽre sǽ),*[11] *that (þæt)*[12] is called Mersea.

	Case	Function
1. **sē here**	nominative	subject
2. **þæs ċeapes**	genitive	
3. **þæs cornes**	genitive	
4. **hīe**	nominative	
5. **þǽre herehȳðe**	dative	
6. **Norðhymbra**	genitive	
7. **lond**	accusative	
8. **sēo fird**	nominative	
9. **hīe**	accusative	
10. **an īġland**	accusative	
11. **þǽre sǽ**	dative	
12. **þæt**	nominative	

3.6 OLD ENGLISH NOUNS (§41)

The three declensions of nouns that appear in Baugh and Cable account for about 70 percent of the nouns that you will encounter in Old English texts: the masculine *a*-stem, or strong masculine, as in *stān* (about 35 percent); the feminine *ō*-stem, or strong feminine, as in *ġiefu* (about 25 percent); and the masculine consonant-stem, or weak masculine, as in *hunta* (about 10 percent).[6] (The stem endings, *a* and *ō*, occurred in Germanic but not in Old English.) Three additional nouns that illustrate these declensions are *cyning, wund,* and *oxa.*

		Strong Masculine	Strong Feminine	Weak Masculine[7]
Singular	N.	cyning 'king'	wund 'wound'	ox-a 'ox'
	G.	cyning-es	wund-e	ox-an
	D.	cyning-e	wund-e	ox-an
	A.	cyning	wund-e	ox-an
Plural	N.	cyning-as	wund-a	ox-an
	G.	cyning-a	wund-a	ox-ena
	D.	cyning-um	wund-um	ox-um
	A.	cyning-as	wund-a	ox-an

A fourth important declension is the neuter *a*-stem, or strong neuter, which includes about 25 percent of Old English nouns. This group is subdivided according to whether the stem is short or long (see question 1 on page 32).

		Strong Neuter (Short Stem)	Strong Neuter (Long Stem)
Singular	N.	scip 'ship'	scēap 'sheep'
	G.	scip-es	scēap-es
	D.	scip-e	scēap-e
	A.	scip	scēap
Plural	N.	scip-u	scēap
	G.	scip-a	scēap-a
	D.	scip-um	scēap-um
	A.	scip-u	scēap

Finally there are a few minor and irregular declensions: mutated plurals (*fōt* 'foot'), *-ru* plurals (*ǣġ* 'egg'), nouns of relationship (*fæder* 'father'), and others.

		Mutated Plurals	-ru Plurals	Nouns of Relationship
Singular	N.	fōt 'foot'	ǣġ 'egg'	fæder 'father'
	G.	fōt-es	ǣġ-es	fæder
	D.	fēt	ǣġ-e	fæder
	A.	fōt	ǣġ	fæder

[6]These percentages are from Randolph Quirk and C. L. Wrenn, *An Old English Grammar* (New York: Holt, Rinehart & Winston, 1957), pp. 19–20.

[7]To the weak masculine nouns should be added the weak feminine nouns, which account for another five percent of all nouns. These differ from weak masculines only in having an *e* in the nominative singular, for example, *eorðe* 'earth'. There are only two weak neuter nouns, *ēage* 'eye' and *ēare* 'ear'.

		Mutated Plurals	-ru Plurals	Nouns of Relationship
Plural	N.	fēt	ǣġ-(e)ru	fæder-as
	G.	fōt-a	ǣġ-(e)ra	fæder-a
	D.	fōt-um	ǣġ-(e)rum	fæder-um
	A.	fēt	ǣġ-(e)ru	fæder-as

Refer to the foregoing paradigms as necessary to answer the following questions.

1. A syllable is short if it contains a short vowel (or short diphthong) followed by a single consonant. A syllable is long if it contains either (i) a long vowel (or long diphthong) or (ii) a short vowel (or short diphthong) followed by more than one consonant. Tell whether the following neuter nouns belong to the short-stem or long-stem declension.

_____ word 'word'   _____ bān 'bone'

_____ fæt 'vessel'   _____ lim 'limb'

_____ hors 'horse'   _____ swīn 'swine'

2. In which two endings do the long-stem neuter nouns differ from the short-stem neuter nouns?

_____

3. Note that the paradigms for the short neuter nouns (both short- and long-stem) are similar to the paradigm for the strong masculine nouns. In which endings are they different? _____

4. Old English *dēor* 'deer' (nominative singular) had the form *dēor* in the nominative and accusative plural. Which of the above declensions does it follow in its unchanged plural? _____

5. The Early Modern English nouns *sheep, horse,* and *ox* had plurals without *-s,* as in Shakespeare's lines (written about 1590):

> Sheepe run not halfe so trecherous from the Wolfe,
> Or Horse or Oxen from the Leopard,
> As you flye from your oft-subdued slaues.

[*1 Henry VI* 1.5.30–32]

Sheepe and *horse* follow the Old English declension in which the nominative and accusative plural remain unchanged. Which declension is this? _____

Ox follows the Old English declension in which an *n* is added in the pural. Which declension is this?_____

6. Old English *fisc* 'fish' had the form *fiscas* in the nominative and accusative plural. To which of the above declensions did it belong in Old English? _____

Which declension is its usual plural modeled on now? _____

7. Old English *scōh* 'shoe' followed the strong masculine declension in its nominative and accusative plural *(scōs),* but its genitive plural was *scōna,* with an *n.* Which declension did the genitive plural follow? _____

8. The plural of *shoe* in the speech of Shakespeare's Cade is *shooen:* "Spare none, but such as go in clouted shooen" (*2 Henry VI* 4.2.195), written about 1590. Notice in the preceding question that *scōh* had an *n* only in the genitive plural. Here the weak declension has generalized to other cases. We shall see in Chapter 7 (§113) that this direction of change was unusual. Which Old English declension does *shoe* in Present-day English ultimately follow? _____

9. Which paradigm do the Modern English forms *tooth/teeth* follow? What other Modern English words form their plurals according to this paradigm?

_____

10. Modern English *child* has a double plural, *children.* Examine the nominative and accusative forms of the paradigms above to determine the two sources of the Modern English ending *-ren.* One source accounts for the *r,* the other for the *n.*

_____

3.7 NOUNS IN SENTENCES (§41)

Examine the italicized Old English nouns for case, number, and function Refer to the paradigms above (§3.6) for help in determining case and number. Section 3.5 lists the grammatical functions of the various cases.

1. Ond þā ġefeaht *sē cyning* Æþerēd wiþ *þāra cyninga* ġetruman.
And then fought the king Æthelred against the kings' troops.

sē cyning: Case __N__ Number __Sg__ Function __Subject__

þāra cyninga: Case _____ Number _____ Function _____

2. Norþhymbre and Ēastengle hæfdon Ælfrēde *cyninge* āþas ġeseald.
Northumbrians and East-Angles had Alfred king oaths given.

Case _____ Number _____ Function _____

3. Hē mid gāre stang wlancne wīċing þe him *þā wunde* forġeaf.
He with spear stabbed bold viking who him the wound gave.

Case _____ Number _____ Function _____

4. Wīġend crungon *wundum* wērġe.
Warriors fell (by) wounds exhausted.

Case _____ Number _____ Function _____

5. Iċ bōhte ān ġetȳme *oxena.*
   I   bought a   team (of) oxen.

   Case _____   Number _____   Function _____

6. Ðā ġenam Abimelech *oxan* and *scēp.*
   Then took   Abimelech   oxen and sheep.

   oxan: Case _____   Number _____   Function _____

   scep (= sceap):   Case _____   Number _____   Function _____

7. And þa *scēap* ġehȳrað his stefne.
   And the sheep hear   his voice.

   Case _____   Number _____   Function _____

8. Ġē ne synt of mīnum *scēapum.*
   Ye not are among my   sheep.

   Case _____   Number _____   Function _____

9. Hwylċ man is of ēow þe hæfð hund *scēapa?*
   Which one is among you who has a hundred sheep?

   Case _____   Number _____   Function _____

10. And on *scyp* stīġende hī fōron onsundran on wēste stōwe.
    And on ship moving   they went privately   to barren place.

    Case _____   Number _____   Function _____

11. þā men of Lundenbyriġ ġefetodon þā *scipu.*
    Those men of London   fetched   the ships.

    Case _____   Number _____   Function _____

12. Ond þǣr forwearþ cxx *scipa* æt Swānawīċ.
    And there perished 120 ships   at Swanage.

    Case _____   Number _____   Function _____

13. Ċealde ġeþrungen wǣron mīne *fēt.*
    By cold pinched   were   my feet.

    Case _____   Number _____   Function _____

14. Stincende āttor singāllīċe of ðām tōswollenum *fōtum* flēow.
    Stinking   poison continuously from the swollen   feet   flowed.

    Case _____   Number _____   Function _____

15. Oððe ġyf hē bit *ǣġ,* segst þū rǣcð hē him scorpionem?
    Or   if he requests egg, say'st thou he gives him   scorpion?

    Case _____   Number _____   Function _____

16. Selle mon uuēġe cǣsa, ond fisces, ond butran, ond *ǣgera.*
    Give one a weight of cheeses, and fish   and butter,   and eggs.

    Case _____   Number _____   Function _____

3.8 OLD ENGLISH ADJECTIVES (§43)

Old English adjectives took the *weak* inflectional endings if a definite article or possessive pronoun preceded and the *strong* inflectional endings if no such word was present. The adjectives in the following sentences are marked for case, number, and gender. (The abbreviation gpm stands for genitive plural masculine; nsn for nominative singular neuter, etc.) The full paradigms for the strong and weak declensions are given in Baugh and Cable §43. Circle Strong or Weak, and supply the appropriate ending if an ending is needed. (Two of the adjectives will not require an ending.)

1. Þā stōd sē earming ǣtforan þām ārlēas-_____ (dsm) dēofle.
   Then stood the wretch   before   the   cruel   devil.

   Strong   Weak

2. Hēo ne rōhte his worda for þǣra wōdlic-_____ (dsf) ontendnysse.
   She did not care about his words because of the mad   passion.

   Strong   Weak

3. Byrhtnōþ maðelode, bord hafenode, wand wāc-_____ (asm) æsc.
   Byrhtnoth   spoke,   shield raised,   waved slender   spear.

   Strong   Weak

4. Hēo on flet ġecrong—sweord wæs swātiġ-_____ (nsn).
   She on floor died—   sword   was bloody.

   Strong   Weak

5. Wēan oft ġehēt earm-_____ (dsf) teohhe ondlong-_____ (asf) niht.
   Woe often (he) vowed (to) wretched   band   entire   night.

   earm-:   Strong   Weak

   ondlong-:   Strong   Weak

6. Ōswold oferwann þone wælhrēow-_____ (asm) cynincg.
   Oswold defeated   the   cruel   king.

   Strong   Weak

7. Þā bær man þām cyninge cynelīc-_____ (apm) þēnunga on ānum
   Then bore one (to) the king   royal   services on a
                                                       of food

   sylfrenan disce.
   silver   dish.

   Strong   Weak

8. Hāma ætwæġ tō þǣre byrht-_____ (dsf) byriġ Brōsinga mene.
   Hama carried off to the bright   city Brosings' necklace.

   Strong   Weak

9. Ongann ċeallian þā ofer ċeald-_____ (dsn) wæter Byrhthelmes bearn.
   <small>Began   to call   then over cold   water   Byrhthelm's   son.</small>

   Strong   Weak

10. Hē hine ætbrǣd þām flǣsclīc-_____ (dpm) lustum.
    <small>He himself refrained from the fleshly   desires.</small>

    Strong   Weak

11. Ond þǣr wearþ Hēahmund bisceop ofslæġen, ond fela gōd-_____ (gpm)
    <small>And there   was   Heahmund   bishop   slain,   and   many good</small>
    monna.
    <small>men.</small>

    Strong   Weak

12. Ac hine sē hālga wer gyrde grǣg-_____ (isn) sweorde.
    <small>But himself the holy man girded (with) gray   sword.</small>

    Strong   Weak

13. Þā ēode hē furður oð hē ġemette ðā gram-_____ (apf) gydena.
    <small>Then went he further   until he found   the angry   goddesses.</small>

    Strong   Weak

14. Þū eart mæġenes strang-_____ (nsm), ond on mōde frōd.
    <small>Thou art of might   strong,   and   in   mind   wise.</small>

    Strong   Weak

3.9 OLD ENGLISH PRONOUNS (§45)

Beside each Old English personal pronoun, write the Modern English pronoun, if any, that has derived from it. The Modern English form may be exactly the same as the Old English, or it may reflect phonological changes. If the Old English pronoun has not survived into Modern English—either because a loanword or an analogical form has replaced it or because a grammatical distinction was lost—write "0". You can check the Old English forms of your proposed Modern English words in a collegiate dictionary, where the Old English form should appear in the etymology. Part of the chart is filled in. Complete the rest.

		1st Person		2nd Person		3rd Person M		F		N	
Singular	N. iċ	*I*	ðū	*thou*	hē	*he*	hēo	*0*	hit	*it*
	G. mīn		ðīn		his		hiere		his	
	D. mē		ðē		him		hiere		him	
	A. mē		ðē		hine		hīe		hit	

Figure 3.3

Dual	N. wit	0	ġit	0
	G. uncer		incer	
	D. unc		inc	
	A. unc		inc	

Plural	N. wē		ġē		hīe	
	G. ūre		ēower		hiera	
	D. ūs		ēow		him	
	A. ūs		ēow		hīe	

Figure 3.3 *(cont.)*

3.10 OLD ENGLISH STRONG VERBS (§46)

1. From the principal parts of the strong verbs in Baugh and Cable §46, write the vowels and diphthongs that occur in the roots (the first vowel or diphthong).

Class	Infinitive	Preterite Singular	Preterite Plural	Past Participle
I	ī	ā	i	i
II	___	___	___	___
III	___	___	___	___
IV	___	___	___	___
V	___	___	___	___
VI	___	___	___	___
VII	___	___	___	___

2. Use the above table to complete the principal parts of the following strong verbs. The infinitive ending is *-an,* as given; the preterite indicative third-person singular has no ending; the preterite indicative plural ending is *-on;* the past participle ending is *-en.* Below the Old English forms give the past tense and past participle in Modern English. The forms of *bītan* have been filled in as an example.

Infinitive	Preterite Singular	Preterite Plural	Past Participle
bītan (I)	bāt	biton	biten
'bite'	bit		bitten or bit
healdan (VII)			
'hold'			
teran (IV)			
'tear'			
meltan (III)			
'melt'			
stelan (IV)			
'steal'			
tredan (V)			
'tread'			
rīdan (I)			
'ride'			
dragan (VI)			
'draw'			
scēotan (II)			
'shoot'			
swellan (III)			
'swell'			
wefan (V)			
'weave'			
wrītan (I)			
'write'			

3.11 OLD ENGLISH SYNTAX AND METER (§51)

English is known as a "stress-timed" language, which means that varying numbers of unstressed syllables occur before and after stressed syllables, and yet the stressed syllables are perceived as occurring at approximately equal intervals of time. The tight control of Old English meter allows us to see this feature of the English language at its earliest period. One way of thinking about the meter of Old English is as a series of four positions:

```
 1   2   3   4
┌───┬───┬───┬───┐
│ x │ / │ \ │ x │
└───┴───┴───┴───┘
```

in gēardagum

in yore-days

Usually each position is filled by a single syllable, but there is an option that allows for expansion: either of the first two positions (but not both) may be filled by more than one *unstressed* syllable. In the following verses from *Beowulf,* all of the unmarked syllables in the first or second position are metrically unstressed. Put an x over each of these syllables (remembering that final *-e* is pronounced in Old English) and write the number of consecutive unstressed syllables in the blank indicated.[8]

Example:

```
┌─────┬───┬───┐
│ x x │ / │ x │ /
└─────┴───┴───┘
```
Unstressed syllables: _2_

1.   þā se wyrm onwōc   (2287a)

When the dragon woke

Conj Art N   V

```
┌───────┬───┬───┐
│       │ / │ x │ /
└───────┴───┴───┘
```
Unstressed syllables:___

2.   ða wæs Heregār dēad   (467b)

Then was Heregar dead

Adv Cop   N   Adj

```
┌───┬───────┬───┐
│ / │       │ / │ x
└───┴───────┴───┘
```
Unstressed syllables:___

3.   Ða wæs on morgen   (837a)

Then was in morning

Adv V Prep   N

---

[8]The justification for the marking of stressed and unstressed syllables as they appear here is beyond our present concern—a subject of its own that is a topic of continuing controversy (for example, why the adverb *ðā* is marked as stressed in #3, which otherwise would have only three positions, but is unstressed in #2). See Thomas Cable, *The English Alliterative Tradition* (Philadelphia: Univ. of Pennsylvania Press, 1991), pp. 6–40.

4.

		/	x	/

þǣr he hine ǣr forlēt

where he him before left

Conj Pro Pro   Adv   V

Unstressed syllables:___

(2787b)

5.

		/	x	/

þǣr   him hel onfēng

There him hell received

Adv   Pro N   V

Unstressed syllables:___

(852b)

6.

	/		/	x

Ðǣr wæs on blōde

There   was   in blood

Adv   Aux Prep N

Unstressed syllables:___

(847a)

7.

		/	/	x

þonne hē on þæt   sinc starað

when   he on that treasure stares

Conj   Pro Prep Art N   V

Unstressed syllables:___

(1485b)

8.

		/	/	x

þonne se weard swefeð

Then   the guardian sleeps

Adv   Art   N   V

Unstressed syllables:___

(1741b)

9.

	/		/	x

þonne cwið æt beore

Then   says at beer

Adv   V   Prep N

Unstressed syllables:___

(2041a)

		/	/	x

Unstressed syllables:___

10.   swā hīe oft ǣr dydon   (1238b)

As they oft before did

Conj Pro Adv Adv V

		/	/	x

Unstressed syllables:___

11.   Swā sceal man do(a)n   (1534a)

So   shall (a) man do

Adv Aux   N   Inf

/			/	x

Unstressed syllables:___

12.   Swā hē ne forwyrnde   (1142a)

So   he not disdained

Adv Pro Neg   V

		/	/	x

Unstressed syllables:___

13.   Hæfdon swurd nacod   (539a)

Had   sword naked

V   N   Adj

		/	x	/

Unstressed syllables:___

14.   sealde his hyrsted sweord   (672b)

gave   his adorned sword

V   Pro   PP   N

The abbreviations beneath the glosses stand for the following grammatical categories:

N	Noun	Aux	Auxiliary Verb
Adj	Adjective	Cop	Copula (linking verb *be*)
Inf	Infinitive	Conj	Conjunction
PP	Past Participle	Prep	Preposition
V	Finite Lexical Verb	Art	Definite Article
Adv	Adverb	Neg	Negative Particle

1. From the information in the examples above, list the grammatical categories that are always stressed:

Stressed Words

_____

_____

_____

_____

2. List the grammatical categories that are always unstressed:

Unstressed Words

_____

_____

_____

_____

_____

_____

3. List the two categories that can be either stressed or unstressed.[9]

Variable Words

_____

_____

[9]The three groups that result from this classification correspond roughly to the categories in a well-known system known as Kuhn's Laws: Stressed Words = Kuhn's Stressed Words; Unstressed Words = Kuhn's Proclitics; Variable Words = Kuhn's Particles. The basic work is Hans Kuhn, "Zur Wortstellung und -betonung im Altgermanischen," *Beiträge zur Geschichte der deutschen Sprache und Literatur,* 57 (1933), 1–109. A more complete study would show that Unstressed Words can sometimes be stressed. An even more complete study might argue that the meter does much of the work that Kuhn attributes to his laws. See Mary Blockley and Thomas Cable, "Kuhn's Laws, Old English Poetry, and the New Philology," in *Beowulf: Essential Articles,* ed. Peter Baker (New York: Garland, 1993).

4. Notice that the first twelve examples all begin with a conjunction or an adverb. List each initial *conjunction* and its Modern English translation:

Old English   Modern English

_____   _____

_____   _____

_____   _____

_____   _____

5. List each initial *adverb* and its Modern English translation:

Old English   Modern English

_____   _____

_____   _____

_____   _____

_____   _____

3.12 THE LANGUAGE ILLUSTRATED (§47)

Ælfric

The West Saxon translation of the account of Moses and the Red Sea is from the work known as *Ælfric's Heptateuch*. The most prolific and learned writer of his age, Abbot Ælfric (c. 955–c. 1012) is especially known for the grace, art, and lucidity of his prose style. Although his actual share in the Old Testament translations from the fourth-century Latin Vulgate is uncertain, we have his own testimony that he translated the crossing of the Israelites through the Red Sea.[10]

[10]Reprinted by permission of the Council of the Early English Text Society from *The Old English Version of the Heptateuch, Ælfric's Treatise on the Old and New Testament, and his Preface to Genesis,* ed. S. J. Crawford, EETS OS 160 (London, 1922), pp. 250–51.

Moses and the Red Sea
Exodus 14:21–31

Ðā Moyses āðenode his hand ofer ðā sǣ ðā sende Drihten miċelne wind ealle
When Moses stretched   out his hand over the sea then sent the Lord great   wind all

ðā niht and ġewende ðā sǣ tō drīum; and þæt wæter wearð on twā tōdǣled, and
the night and   turned   the sea to dry land; and   that   water   became in two divided,   and

lǣġ ān drīge strǣt ðurh ðā sǣ. And ðæt wæter stōd on twā healfa ðǣre strǣte
lay a dry   street through the sea. And the   water stood on   two sides   of the street

swylċe twēġen hēaġe weallas: ðā fōr eall Ysrahela folc ðurh ðā sǣ on þone weġ ðe
like   two   high   walls;   then went all Israel's   folk through the sea on the   way which

Drihten him ġeworhte, and ðā cōmon hāle and ġesunde þurh ðā sǣ, swā Drihten
the Lord for them made,   and they came whole and sound   through the sea, as   the Lord

him behēt. Ðā Pharao cōm tō ðǣre sǣ, and eal his here, ðā fōr hē on þone ylcan
them promised. When Pharaoh came to the   sea, and all his army, then went he on the   same

weġ æfter Israhela folce on dæġrēd mid eallum his folce and mid eallum his wǣpnum.
way after Israel's   people at daybreak with all   his people and with all   his weapons.

Ðā cwæð Drihten tō Moyse: Āðene ðīne hand ofer ðā sǣ and ofer Faraon and ofer
Then said the Lord to Moses: Stretch out thine hand over the sea and over Pharoah and over

ealne his here. And hē āhefde ūp his hand, and sēo sǣ slōh tōgædere and āhwylfde
all   his army. And he raised up his hand, and the sea struck together   and covered

Pharaones cratu, and ādrenċte hine sylfne and eal his folc, þæt ðǣr ne wearð furðon ān
Pharaoh's carts and drowned   himsef   and all his people so that there not remained even one

tō lāfe þe līf ġebyrede. Sōðliċe Moyses and Israhela folc fōron ðurh ðā sǣ
whom   life belonged to. Truly   Moses   and Israel's   people went through the sea

drīum fōtum. And Drihten ālȳsde on ðām dæġe Israhela folc of ðǣra
with dry feet.   And the Lord   freed   on that day   Israel's people from the

Egyptiscra handum. And hi ġesawon þā Egyptiscan dēade ūp tō lande āworpene,
Egyptians' hands.   And they saw   the Egyptians   dead up on land thrown

þe heora ǣr ēhton on ðam lande þe hi ðā tō cumene wǣron: and ðæt Israhelisce
who them earlier pursued on the land   which they   had come to: and that Israelite

folc ondrēdon him Drihten and hȳdron Gode and Moyses his ðēowe.
people feared   the Lord and heard (obeyed) God and Moses   his servant.

West Saxon Gospels

The translation known as the *West Saxon Gospels,* from about the beginning of the eleventh century, was one of the results of the Benedictine Reform (Baugh and Cable §63). In its original form, which has not survived, the West Saxon version was a continuous gloss of the Latin Vulgate. In the surviving manuscripts the translation is in straight idiomatic prose that remains fairly faithful to the original.[11]

The Nativity
Luke 2.1–14

Sōþlīċe on þām dagum wæs ġeworden ġebod fram þām cāsere Augusto, þæt eall
Verily in those days was made a command by the emperor Augustus, that all

ymbehwyrft wǣre tōmearcod. Þēos tōmearcodnes wæs ǣryst ġeworden fram þām
the world be enumerated. This census was first made by the

dēman Syriġe Cirino. And ealle hiġ ēodon, and syndriġe fērdon on hyra
ruler of Syria Cyrenius. And all they proceeded, and separately went to their

ċeastre. Ðā fērde Iosep fram Galilea of þǣre ċeastre Nazareth on Iudeisce ċeastre
city. Then went Joseph from Galilee from the city Nazareth into the Judaic city

Dauides, sēo is ġenemned Bethleem, for þām þe hē wæs of Dauides hūse and
of David, which is named Bethlehem, because he was of David's house and

hīrede; þæt hē fērde mid Marian þe him beweddod wæs, and wæs ġeēacnod.
family; so that he went with Mary who to him wedded was, and was with child.

Sōþlīċe wæs ġeworden þā hī þār wǣron, hire dagas wǣron ġefyllede þæt hēo cende.
Verily was come to pass while they there were, her days were fulfilled that she gave birth.

And hēo cende hyre frumcennedan sunu, and hine mid ċildclāþum bewand, and
And she bore her first-born son and him with swaddling-clothes wrapped, and

hine on binne ālēde, for þām þe hiġ næfdon rūm on cumena hūse. And hyrdas wǣron
him in a manger laid, because they did not have room in guests' house. And shepherds were

on þām ylcan rīċe waciende, and nihtwæċċan healdende ofer heora heorda. Þā stōd
in the same country keeping awake, and nightwatch holding over their herds. Then stood

Drihtnes engel wiþ hiġ, and Godes beorhtnes him ymbe scēan; and hī him
the Lord's angel beside them, and God's brightness them around shone; and they for themselves

myċelum eġe ādrēdon. And sē engel him tō cwæð, Nelle ġē ēow ādrǣdan;
with great awe feared. And the angel to them said, Do not ye fear for yourselves;

sōþlīċe nū iċ ēow bodie myċelne ġefēan, sē bið eallum folce; for þām tō
verily now I to you proclaim great joy, which is to all people; for

dæġ ēow ys Hǣlend ācenned, sē is Drihten Crīst, on Dauides ċeastre. And þis tācen
today to you is a Savior born, who is Lord Christ, in David's city. And this sign

ēow byð: Ġē ġemētað ān ċild hræġlum bewunden, and on binne ālēd. And þā
to you is: Ye will find a child in cloths wrapped, and in manger laid. And then

wæs fǣringa ġeworden mid þām engle myċelnes heofonlīċes werydes, God heriendra
was suddenly come about with the angel great heavenly host, God praising

[11]From James W. Bright, ed., *The Gospel of Saint Luke in West-Saxon* (Boston: Heath, 1906), pp. 10–12.

and þus cweþendra, Gode sȳ wuldor on hēahnesse, and on eorðan sybb mannum
and thus   saying   to God be glory   in highest,   and on earth   peace to men

gōdes willan.
of good will.

Ohthere's Voyage

In the Alfredian translation of Orosius's *Compendious History of the World,* there is an interpolated geographical text that supplements the original Latin. The new material updates the fifth-century history by reporting the firsthand accounts of two contemporary voyagers, Ohthere and Wulfstan. The prose is of special interest for giving a glimpse of informal English during the late ninth century in a text that is not a translation. The following excerpt tells of Ohthere's voyage around the north coast of Norway into the White Sea.[12]

Ōhthere sǣde his hlāforde, Ælfrede cyninge, þæt hē ealra Norðmonna norþmest
Ohthere told   his lord,   Alfred   king   that he of all   Norsemen   northmost

būde. Hē cwæð þæt hē būde on þǣm lande norþweardum wiþ þā Westsǣ. Hē
lived. He said   that he lived in that   land   northward   along the West Sea. He

sǣde þēah þæt land sīe swīþe lang norþ þonan; ac hit is eal wēste, būton
said however that land is very   far   north thence; but it is all waste,   except that

on fēawum stōwum styċċemǣlum wīciað Finnas, on huntoðe on wintra, ond on
in a few   places   here and there camp   Lapps, in hunting in winter,   and in

sumera on fiscaþe be þǣre sǣ. Hē sǣde þæt hē æt sumum ċirre wolde fandian
summer in fishing along that sea. He said   that he at one   time wanted to see

hū longe þæt land norþryhte lǣġe, oþþe hwæðer æniġ mon be norðan þǣm wēstenne
how far   that land due north extended, or whether any   man   north   of that waste

būde. Þā fōr hē norþryhte be þǣm lande: lēt him ealne weġ þæt wēste
lived. Then went he due north along that   land: kept him all the way that waste

land on ðæt stēorbord, ond þā wīdsǣ on ðæt bæcbord þrīe dagas. Þā wæs hē
land on the starboard,   and the open sea on the port   three days. Then was he

swā fēor norþ swā þā hwælhuntan firrest faraþ. Þā fōr hē þāġīet norþryhte
as   far north as the whale hunters farthest go.   Then went he still due north

swā fēor swā hē meahte on þǣm ōþrum þrim dagum ġesiġlan. Þā bēag þæt
as   far   as he was able in the next   three days   to sail.   Then bent that

land þǣr ēastryhte, oþþe sēo sǣ in on ðæt lond, hē nysse hwæðer, būton hē
land there due east,   or   that sea in on that land, he knew not which,   except that he

wisse ðæt hē ðǣr bād westanwindes ond hwōn norþan, ond siġlde ðā ēast
knew that he there awaited a west wind and slightly from the   north,   and sailed then east

[12]From Henry Sweet, ed., *King Alfred's Orosius,* EETS OS 79 (London, 1883), p. 17.

be lande swā swā hē meahte on fēower dagum ġesiġlan. . . . Ðā
along land as (far) as he was able   in four   days   to sail.   Then

læġ þǣr ān miċel ēa ūp in on þæt land. þā ċirdon hīe ūp in on
extended there a great river inland on that land.   Then turned they ashore   on

ðā ēa, for þǣm hīe ne dorston forþ bī þǣre ēa siġlan for unfriþe,
that river, because they not   dared   forth along that river sail because of hostility,

for þǣm ðæt land wæs eall ġebūn on ōþre healfe þǣre ēas. Ne mētte hē ǣr nān
because   that land   was   all cultivated on other side   of the river. Not found he before no

ġebun land siþþan hē from his āgnum hām fōr. Ac him wæs ealne
cultivated land since   he from   his own   home went. But to him was all the

weġ wēste on þæt stēorbord, būtan fiscerum ond fugelerum ond huntum,
way waste land on the starboard,   except fishers   and fowlers   and hunters,

ond þæt wǣron eall Finnas; ond him wæs ā wīdsǣ on ðæt bæcbord.
and that   were   all Lapps;   and to him was always open sea on the   port.

4

Foreign Influences on Old English

4.1 QUESTIONS FOR REVIEW

1. Explain why the following people and events are important in historical discussions of the English language:

St. Augustine
Bede
Alcuin
Dunstan
Ælfric
Cnut
Treaty of Wedmore
Battle of Maldon

2. Define the following terms:

i-Umlaut
Palatal diphthongization
The Danelaw

3. How extensive was the Celtic influence on Old English?

4. What accounts for the difference between the influence of Celtic and that of Latin upon the English language?

5. During what three periods did Old English borrow from Latin?

6. What event, according to Bede, inspired the mission of St. Augustine? In what year did the mission begin?

7. What were the three periods of Viking attacks on England?

8. What are some of the characteristic endings of place-names borrowed from Danish?

9. About how many Scandinavian place-names have been counted in England?

10. Approximately how many Scandinavian words appeared in Old English?

11. From what language has English acquired the pronouns *they, their, them,* and the present plural *are* of the verb *to be?* What were the equivalent Old English words?

12. What inflectional elements have been attributed to Scandinavian influence?

13. What influence did Christianity have on Old English?

Figure 4.1   England after The Treaty of Wedmore (878).

4.2 DATING LATIN LOANWORDS THROUGH SOUND CHANGES (§57)

In *A History of the English Language,* Baugh and Cable show how sound changes in prehistoric Old English, such as *i-umlaut* and *palatal diphthongization,* can be used to determine the period during which words were borrowed into the language. The examples on pages 52–53 illustrate these principles of relative dating on the basis of *i-umlaut* and another important sound change, *breaking.*

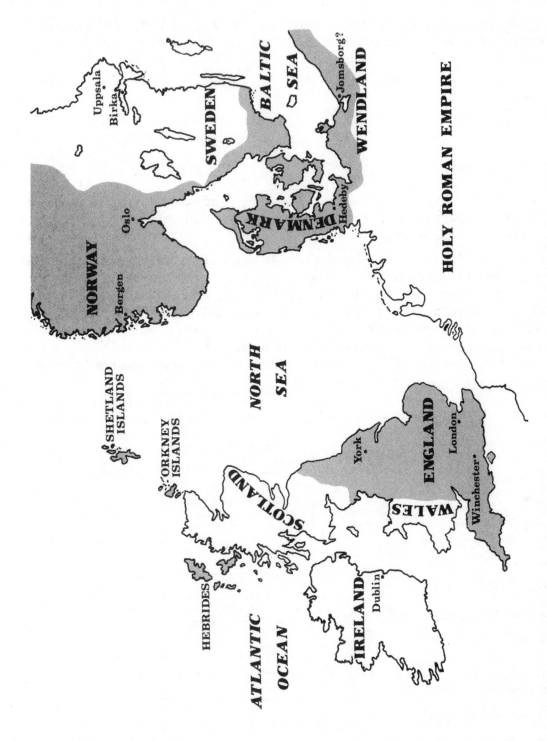

Figure 4.2 The Empire of Cnut (1016–1035). Denmark, England, Norway, and southern Sweden were under the direct rule of Cnut. So also were the Slavic lands along the southern rim of the Baltic Sea, though the boundaries here are vaguer. In addition, Scotland, Wales, and the eastern part of Ireland owed suzerainty to the Danish king and can be considered vassal states.

i-Umlaut

i-Umlaut, or **i-mutation,** causes a back or central vowel to become a front vowel because of the anticipation of an *i* or *j* in the next syllable. (The notation ō̆ > ē̆ means ō > ē and ŏ > ĕ.)

> ă > ĕ
>
> ō̆ > ē̆
>
> ā > ǣ
>
> ŭ > ̆ȳ
>
> ĕa and ĕo > īe

We know that these changes took place before the earliest extant records of Old English, probably during the seventh century. We can deduce that a word that underwent the change must have been in the language at that date.

Examine the Old English and Latin forms of the following words to determine whether *i*-umlaut occurred, and if it did, indicate the change. Because the *i* or *j* that caused umlaut often appeared only in West Germanic and prehistoric Old English, you should compare the vowel of the first syllable of the Old English word with the corresponding vowel of the Latin word (each in bold type). If the vowel did not change, check *Indeterminate* to indicate that additional information is needed to date the entry of the word into English.

For those words that did not undergo *i*-umlaut, what deductions about the date of their entry into English can be drawn from their meanings? _____

_____

Latin	Old English	In OE During i-Umlaut		Vowel Change by i-Umlaut
		Yes	Indeter-minate	
balteus 'girdle'	belt	✓		a > e
puteus 'pit'	pytt			
crēdo 'I believe'	crēda 'creed'			
uncia 'twelfth part'	ynċe 'inch'			
diāconus 'deacon'	diacon			
sagēna 'seine'	seġne			
pulvī-nus 'cushion'	pyle 'pillow'			
sabbatum 'sabbath'	sabat			
Vulg. L. cucīna (variant of *coquīna*, from *coquere* 'to cook')	cyċene 'kitchen'			
strāta 'paved road'	strǣt 'street'			

Breaking

Diphthongs were formed in prehistoric Old English not only by **palatal diphthongization** (Baugh & Cable §57) but also at an earlier date by **breaking** before certain consonants. The vowel *a,* for example, which best illustrates the process in loanwords from Latin, was first fronted to **æ** (by a separate sound change) and then broken to become the diphthong *ea* [æə] whenever it preceded **r** + a consonant, **l** + a consonant, or **h** [x]:

   (i) **a > æ**

   (ii) **æ > ea** when followed by $\begin{cases} \textbf{r} + \text{consonant} \\ \textbf{l} + \text{consonant} \\ \textbf{h} \end{cases}$

Thus, the vowel in the native English word *healf* 'half' was originally [ɑ], which became [æ] and then by breaking [æə]. Any Latin word with [ɑ] and the right consonants would have undergone the same changes if it had been in prehistoric Old English at that date.

   For each of the following words, check *Yes* if it underwent breaking and thus was in the language at the time of the sound change, and check *No* if it had the structure for breaking but did not undergo it and thus was not in the language. If the sound did not have the structure for breaking and therefore cannot be dated by this rule, check *Indeterminate.*[1] (The first word, *vallum,* for example, fits the context for breaking—**l** + the consonant **l**—and the vowel of the Old English word *weall* has become a diphthong; thus, the word was in the language at the time of breaking, and *Yes* is checked. The second word, *falsus,* fits the context for breaking—**l** + the

Latin	Old English	In OE During Breaking		
		Yes	No	Indeter-minate
vallum 'wall'	weall	✓		
falsus 'false'	fals		✓	
arca 'chest'	earc 'ark'			
abbādem (late L.) 'abbot'	abbad			
palma 'palm'	palm			
martyr 'martyr'	martyr			
camēlus 'camel'	camel			
sanctus (p.p. of *sancīre* 'to devote')	sanct 'saint'			
calcem, calx 'lime'	ċealc 'chalk'			
altāre 'high place'	alter 'altar'			
cantor 'singer'	cantere			

[1]The precise date for breaking cannot be established. It would necessarily have been sometime between the Germanic invasion of England in the middle of the fifth century and the oldest surviving texts in the first half of the eighth. The relative chronology of sound changes puts breaking closer to the beginning of that period. See A. Campbell, *Old English Grammar* (Oxford: Oxford University Press, 1959), pp. 50, 109.

consonant **s**—but since the vowel remains unchanged in Old English *fals,* it could not have been in the language during the sound change; thus, *No* is checked.)

4.3 SCANDINAVIAN LOANWORDS (§§72, 75–76)

The following loanwords are borrowings from Old Norse that replaced native words in late Old English or early Middle English. Check each Modern English form in the *Oxford English Dictionary* for the Old Norse word, the Old English word that it replaced, and the form that the Old English word took if it survived into Middle or Modern English. The last item, printed in SMALL CAPITALS after the Old English in the *OED,* will suggest the probable word that we would be using now if it were not for the Scandinavian influence during the Old English period. Look up each word under the first entry for its part of speech—substantive (*sb.*), adjective (*a., adj.*), or verb (*v.*)—as indicated below. All the etymological information that you need is in brackets at the beginning of each entry. (The abbreviation "a. ON" means "adopted from Old Norse.")

Modern English	Old Norse	Native Old English	Development of Old English
Substantives (Nouns)			
loan	lān	lǣn	LEND
race			
scab			
scale			
sister			—
skirt			
swain			
window			
Adjectives			
loose			
low			
weak			
Verbs			
bait			—
call			—
cast			
get			—
raise			

5

The Norman Conquest and the Subjection of English, 1066–1200

5.1 QUESTIONS FOR REVIEW

1. Explain why the following people are important in historical discussions of the English language:

Æthelred
Edward the Confessor
Godwin
Harold
William, duke of Normandy
Henry I
Henry II

2. How would the English language probably have been different if the Norman Conquest had never occurred?

3. From what settlers does Normandy derive its name? When did they come to France?

4. Why did William consider that he had a claim on the English throne?

5. What was the decisive battle between the Normans and the English? How did the Normans win it?

6. When was William crowned king of England? How long did it take him to complete his conquest of England and gain complete recognition? In what parts of the country did he face rebellions?

7. What happened to Englishmen in positions of church and state under William's rule?

8. For how long after the Norman Conquest did French remain the principal language of the upper classes in England?

9. How did William divide his lands at his death?

10. What was the extent of the lands ruled by Henry II and Eleanor of Aquitaine?

11. What was generally the attitude of the French kings and upper classes to the English language?

12. What does the literature written under the patronage of the English court indicate about French culture and language in England during this period?

13. How complete was the fusion of the French and English peoples in England?

14. In general, which parts of the population spoke English, and which French?

15. To what extent did the upper classes learn English? What can one infer concerning Henry II's knowledge of English?

16. How far down in the social scale was a knowledge of French at all general?

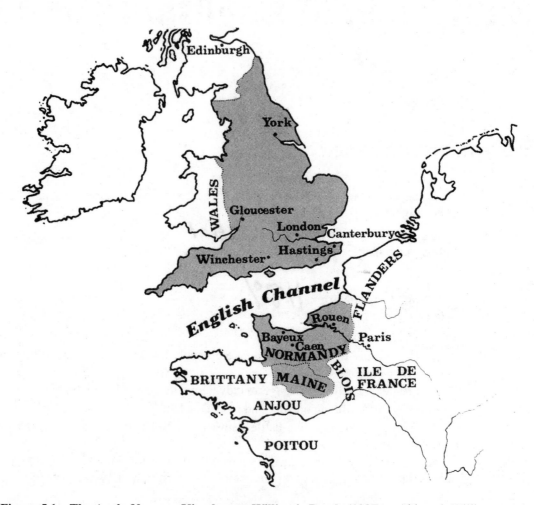

Figure 5.1   The Anglo-Norman Kingdom at William's Death (1087).   Although William acquired Maine by force in 1063, the district remained an area of dispute between Normandy and Anjou throughout his reign. The border between England and Scotland was not determined until William's death.

Figure 5.2   Dominions of Henry II (1154–1189).

6

The Reestablishment of English, 1200–1500

6.1 QUESTIONS FOR REVIEW

1. Explain why the following are important in historical discussions of the English language:

King John
Philip, king of France
Henry III
The Hundred Years' War
The Black Death
The Peasants' Revolt
Statute of Pleading
Layamon
Geoffrey Chaucer
John Wycliffe

2. In what year did England lose Normandy? What events brought about the loss?

3. What effect did the loss of Normandy have upon the nobility of France and England and consequently upon the English language?

4. Despite the loss of Normandy, what circumstances encouraged the French to continue coming to England during the long reign of Henry III (1216–1272)?

5. The arrival of foreigners during Henry III's reign undoubtedly delayed the spread of English among the upper classes. In what ways did these events actually benefit the English language?

6. What was the status of French throughout Europe in the thirteenth century?

7. What explains the fact that the borrowing of French words begins to assume large proportions during the second half of the thirteenth century, as the importance of the French language in England is declining?

8. What general conclusions can one draw about the position of English at the end of the thirteenth century?

9. What can one conclude about the use of French in the church and the universities by the fourteenth century?

10. What kind of French was spoken in England, and how was it regarded?

11. In what way did the Hundred Years' War probably contribute to the decline of French in England?

12. According to Baugh and Cable, the Black Death reduced the numbers of the lower classes disproportionately and yet indirectly increased the importance of the language that they spoke. Why was this so?

13. What specifically can one say about changing conditions for the middle class in England during the thirteenth and fourteenth centuries? What effect did these changes have upon the English language?

14. In what year was Parliament first opened with a speech in English?

15. What statute marks the official recognition of the English language in England?

16. When did English begin to be used in the schools?

17. What was the status of the French language in England by the end of the fifteenth century?

18. About when did English become generally adopted for the records of towns and the central government?

19. What does English literature between 1150 and 1350 tell us about the changing fortunes of the English language?

20. What do the literary accomplishments of the period between 1350 and 1400 imply about the status of English?

7

Middle English

7.1 QUESTIONS FOR REVIEW

1. Define:

Leveling
Analogy
Anglo-Norman
Central French
Hybrid forms
Latin influence of the Third Period
Aureate diction
Standard English

2. What phonetic changes brought about the leveling of inflectional endings in Middle English?

3. What accounts for the -e in Modern English *stone,* the Old English form of which was *stān* in the nominative and accusative singular?

4. Generally what happened to inflectional endings of nouns in Middle English?

5. What two methods of indicating the plural of nouns remained common in early Middle English?

6. Which form of the adjective became the form for all cases by the close of the Middle English period?

7. What happened to the demonstratives *sē, sēo, þæt* and *þēs, þēos, þis* in Middle English?

8. Why were the losses not so great in the personal pronouns? What distinction did the personal pronouns lose?

9. What is the origin of the *th-* forms of the personal pronoun in the third person plural?

10. What were the principal changes in the verb during the Middle English period?

11. Name five strong verbs that were becoming weak during the thirteenth century.

12. Name five strong past participles that have remained in use after the verb became weak.

13. How many of the Old English strong verbs remain in the language today?

14. What effect did the decay of inflections have upon grammatical gender in Middle English?

15. To what extent did the Norman Conquest affect the grammar of English?

16. In the borrowing of French words into English, how is the period before 1250 distinguished from the period after?

17. Into what general classes do borrowings of French vocabulary fall?

18. What accounts for the difference in pronunciation between words introduced into English after the Norman Conquest and the corresponding words in Modern French?

19. Why are the French words borrowed during the fifteenth century of a bookish quality?

20. What is the period of the greatest borrowing of French words? Altogether about how many French words were adopted during the Middle English period?

21. What principle is illustrated by the pairs *ox/beef, sheep/mutton, swine/pork,* and *calf/veal?*

22. What generally happened to the Old English prefixes and suffixes in Middle English?

23. Despite the changes in the English language brought about by the Norman Conquest, in what ways was the language still English?

24. What was the main source of Latin borrowings during the fourteenth and fifteenth centuries?

25. In which Middle English writers is aureate diction most evident?

26. What tendency may be observed in the following sets of synonyms: *rise—mount—ascend, ask—question—interrogate, goodness—virtue—probity?*

27. What kind of contact did the English have with speakers of Flemish, Dutch, and Low German during the late Middle Ages?

28. What are the five principal dialects of Middle English?

29. Which dialect of Middle English became the basis for Standard English? What causes contributed to the establishment of this dialect?

30. Why did the speech of London have special importance during the late Middle Ages?

7.2 FROM OLD TO MIDDLE ENGLISH: VOWELS[1]

7.2.1 Changes in the Old English Vowels

In the phonological developments from Old English to Middle English, five of the Old English simple vowels changed in quality, and the four Old English diphthongs became simplified to monophthongs.

Sounds		Examples	
Old English	Middle English	Old English	Middle English[2]
1. [ɑ:] > [ɔ:]		bān [ɑ:] >	bǭn [ɔ:] 'bone'
2. [æ] > [ɑ]		þæt [æ] >	that [ɑ] 'that'
3. [æ:][3] > [ɛ:]		sǣ [æ:] >	sę̄ [ɛ:] 'sea'
4. [y] > [ɪ]		synn [y] >	sinne [ɪ] 'sin'
5. [y:] > [i:]		hȳdan [y:] >	hīden [i:] 'hide'
6. [æə] > [ɑ]		hearm [æə] >	harm [ɑ] 'harm'
7. [æ:ə] > [ɛ:]		strēam [æ:ə] >	strę̄me [ɛ:] 'stream'
8. [ɛo] > [ɛ]		heofon [ɛo] >	heven [ɛ] 'heaven'
9. [e:o] > [e:]		bēon [e:o] >	bēn [e:] 'to be'

[1]See Baugh and Cable, Chap. 8, *§175. From Old to Middle English.*
[2]Some modern grammarians use ę and ǫ as below to represent "open e" [ɛ] and "open o" [ɔ], respectively.
[3]This is the [æ:] that resulted from the *i*-umlaut of [ɑ:]. See Baugh and Cable, p. 237.

The Old English words below contain vowels that underwent regular developments in Middle English. The consonants in these words for the most part remained unchanged. Transcribe phonetically the Old English word; then indicate the "stressed vowel change" by writing the number of the appropriate rule from the list of nine changes above; finally, transcribe phonetically the Middle and Modern English forms. Remember that unstressed Old English vowels reduced to [ə] in Middle English. For Modern English do not mark length.

Old English		Stressed Vowel Change	Middle English		Modern English	
hǣþen	[hæːðɛn]	3	hḗþen	[hɛːðən]	heathen	[hiðən]
cræft			craft		craft	
fȳr			fīr		fire	
healf			half		half	
dēop			dēp		deep	
stān			stǭn		stone	
stēap			stḗpe		steep	
cyssan			kisse		kiss	
seofon			seven		seven	
glēo			glē		glee	
dǣl			dḗl		deal	
hāl			hǭl		whole	
ġeolo			yelowe		yellow	
hearpe			harp		harp	
bēatan			bḗten		beat	
sæt			sat		sat	
mȳs			mīs		mice	
fyllan			fillen		fill	

7.2.2 Formation of New Diphthongs

In addition to the changes in the Old English vowels, six new diphthongs appeared in the language. The full history of these diphthongs is complex because of the varied sources from which a single diphthong could derive. Different phonological contexts in Old English resulted in Middle English [ɑʊ], for example, and that diphthong also entered Middle English directly from Old French and Old Norse. The representative sources that are given below for five of the six diphthongs are all of the same phonological type: two separate elements in Old English (simple vowel plus glide or fricative) which merged to produce a single diphthong in Middle English. This is the most important of the contexts that produced the new diphthongs. The sixth diphthong is one that came from French, [ɔɪ], a sound that English still has in *choice, royal, annoy,* etc.

Source	New Diphthong		Examples		
			Old English		Middle English
1. ɑ + w	>	ɑʊ	clawu [klɑwʊ]	>	clawe [klɑʊə] 'claw'
ɑ + ɣ	>	ɑʊ	lagu [lɑɣʊ]	>	lawe [lɑʊə] 'law'
2. æ+ j	>	ɛɪ	dæġ [dæj]	>	dai [dɛɪ] 'day'
ɛ + j	>	ɛɪ	weġ [wɛj]	>	wei [wɛɪ] 'way'
3. ɛ: + w	>	ɛʊ	fēawe [fɛ:wə][4]	>	fewe [fɛʊə] 'few'
4. i: + w	>	ɪʊ	stiweard [sti:wæərd]	>	steward [stɪʊard] 'steward'
5. o: + w	>	oʊ	growan [gro:wɑn]	>	growen [groʊən] 'grow'
ɔ + ɣ	>	oʊ	boga [bɔɣɑ]	>	bowe [boʊə] 'bow'
ɑ: + ɣ	>	oʊ	āgan [ɑ:ɣɑn]	>	owen [oʊən] 'to possess'
6. From Old French	>	ɔɪ	OF joie	>	ME joie 'joy'

The Middle English forms of the words below contain diphthongs that resulted from a merger of phonological elements that were distinct in Old English. Show the historical development by writing the phonetic symbols for the separate Old English sounds and resulting new Middle English diphthong.

Old English	Middle English	Historical Development
glowan [glo:wɑn] 'to glow'	glowe [gloʊə]	[o:] + [w] > [oʊ]
dragan [drɑɣɑn] 'to draw'	drawen [drɑʊən]	[ ] + [ ] > [ ]
fæġer [fæjɛr] 'fair'	fair [fɛɪr]	[ ] + [ ] > [ ]
snīwan [sni:wɑn] 'to snow'	snywen [snɪʊən]	[ ] + [ ] > [ ]
scēawian [šɛ:wɪɑn][5] 'to show'	schewen [šɛʊən]	[ ] + [ ] > [ ]
reġn [rɛjn] 'rain'	rein [rɛɪn]	[ ] + [ ] > [ ]
þawian [θɑwɪɑn] 'to thaw'	thawen [θɑʊən]	[ ] + [ ] > [ ]
næġl [næjl] 'nail'	nail [nɛɪl]	[ ] + [ ] > [ ]
gnagan [gnɑɣɑn] 'to gnaw'	gnawen [gnɑʊən]	[ ] + [ ] > [ ]
flogen [flɔɣɛn] 'flown'	flowen [floʊən]	[ ] + [ ] > [ ]

7.2.3 Lengthening and Shortening

The changes in quantity that vowels underwent in late Old English and early Middle English had far-reaching effects on the history of English and its current phonology. Historically, there were three main developments of stressed vowels, the first and third involving lengthening, the second shortening:

   **1. Lengthening in late Old English before the consonant clusters *ld, mb, nd.* Thus OE *ċild* [čɪld] 'child' became ME *child* [či:ld]. But lengthening did not occur if a third consonant followed: *children* [čɪldrən].

---

[4]This vowel was originally the diphthong [æ:ə], which became [ɛ:] in early Middle English (see the seventh change listed in §7.2.1, above).

[5]See footnote 4.

2. Shortening in early Middle English

a. Before double consonants and consonant clusters, except the clusters that caused lengthening as listed above. Thus OE *cēpte* [keːptɛ] 'he kept' became ME *kept* [kɛpt].

b. In the first syllable of trisyllabic words. Thus OE *hāliġdæġ* [haːlɪjdæj] 'holiday' became ME *halidai* [hɑlɪdɛɪ].

3. Lengthening of *a, e,* and *o* in open syllables of disyllabic words. (Open syllables end in a vowel. In disyllabic words a single consonant between the vowels goes with the second syllable and leaves the first syllable open; two or more consonants make the syllable closed—as in Old English heavy and light syllables, §3.6.1.) Thus OE *nama* [nɑmɑ] 'name' became ME *nāme* [nɑːmə].

The distinction between long and short vowels has developed in Modern English into a distinction between tense vowels (including the diphthongs [aɪ], [aʊ], and [ɔɪ]) and lax vowels (see §0.4.8).

The effect of lengthening can be seen in Modern English words such as *hate* with a "silent -*e*," which in Middle English was pronounced [ə], in contrast with words without the historically open syllable, such as *hat*.

1. In each pair of words below, the stressed vowel in one word changed in quantity between Old English and Middle English, the other did not. The phonetic transcription for the Middle English word is provided. Transcribe the early Old English and the Modern English words and indicate the change, if any, in the *quantity* of the vowel in Middle English by writing the appropriate number in the blank. If there was no change in quantity, write a dash. For Modern English do not mark length.

   1. Lengthening before *ld, mb, nd*
   2. Shortening before consonant cluster
   3. Lengthening in open syllable

	Early Old English	Middle English	Change in Quantity		Modern English
1. a. þēoft	[θeːoft]	theft [θɛft]	2	theft	[θɛft]
b. þēof	[θeːof]	þēf [θeːf]	—	thief	[θif]
2. a. nosu	_____	nǭse [nɔːzə]	_____	nose	_____
b. nosðirl	_____	nǫsthirl [nɔsθɪrl]	_____	nostril	_____
3. a. cēpte	_____	kepte [kɛptə]	_____	kept	_____
b. cēpan	_____	kēpen [keːpən]	_____	keep	_____
4. a. behindan	_____	behīnde [bəhiːndə]	_____	behind	_____
b. hindrian	_____	hindre [hɪndr]	_____	hinder	_____
5. a. læfde	_____	lafte [lɑftə]	_____	left	_____
b. læfan	_____	lēven [lɛːvən]	_____	leave	_____
6. a. blēdde	_____	bledde [blɛddə]	_____	bled	_____
b. blēdan	_____	blēde [bleːdə]	_____	bleed	_____

Early Old English		Middle English	Change in Quantity	Modern English	
7. a. late	_____	lāte [lɑ:tə]	_____	late	_____
b. lǣtera	_____	latere [lɑtərə]	_____	latter	_____
8. a. hund	_____	hound [hu:nd]	_____	hound	_____
b. hundred	_____	hundred [hʊndrəd]	_____	hundred	_____

2. In the column for Modern English above, there are regular alternations between the vowels (or diphthongs) that were originally long [ɑɪ, e, i, ɑʊ, o] and those that have always been short [ɪ, æ, ɛ, ə, ɑ]: [ɑɪ] ~ [ɪ] in item 4 of the above list, [e] ~ [æ] in item 7, [ɛ] ~ [i] in item 1, [ɑʊ] ~ [ə] in item 8, [o] ~ [ɑ] in item 2, etc. Some phonologists have argued that the rule-governed alternations between tense and lax vowels are still productive in English, as illustrated by the words below and words derived from them.[6] Write a phonetic transcription of the tense vowel or diphthong. Supply a related word with a lax vowel, and write a phonetic transcription of its vowel.[7]

Word with Tense Vowel or Diphthong	Modern English Tense Vowel or Diphthong	Related Word with Lax Vowel	Modern English Lax Vowel
derive	[ɑɪ]	derivative	[ɪ]
line	_____	_____	_____
profane	_____	_____	_____
explain	_____	_____	_____
meter	_____	_____	_____
appeal	_____	_____	_____
denounce	_____	_____	_____
verbose	_____	_____	_____

7.3 FROM OLD TO MIDDLE ENGLISH: CONSONANTS (§175)

Consonants changed less than vowels between Old English and Middle English. Some of the most important of the consonant changes are illustrated in the words below. Examine the words from both periods of the language and complete the second halves of the historical rules that follow. If a sound was lost, write Ø.

[6]See Noam Chomsky and Morris Halle, *The Sound Pattern of English* (New York: Harper and Row, 1968), especially Chaps. 4 and 6.

[7]The full relationship of these forms will become clear with the discussion of the Great Vowel Shift in Chap. 8.

Old English	Middle English
hlud [hluːd] 'loud'	lud [luːd]
hlǣne [hlæːnɛ] 'lean'	leane [lɛːnə]
hnecca [hnɛkkɑ] 'neck'	necke [nɛkə]
hnutu [hnʊtʊ] 'nut'	nute [nʊtə]
hring [hrɪŋg] 'ring'	ring [rɪŋg]
hrōf [hroːf] 'roof'	rof [roːf]
swētan [sweːtan] 'sweet' (weak)	swete [sweːtə]
rihtlič [rɪxtlɪč] 'rightly'	rightly [rɪxtlɪ]
ānlič [ɑːnlɪč] 'only'	onli [ɔːnlɪ]
swuster [swʊstɛr] 'sister'	suster [sʊstər]
fæder [fædɛr] 'father'	vader [vɑdər] (South of the Thames)
self [sɛlf] 'self'	zelf [zɛlf] (South of the Thames)

Old English		Middle English
[hl, hn, hr]	>	_____
[n] after unstressed vowel	>	_____
[č] after unstressed vowel	>	_____
[w] after consonant and before back vowel	>	_____
Initial [f, s] (South of the Thames)	>	_____

7.4 FROM OLD ENGLISH TO MIDDLE ENGLISH: VOWEL REDUCTION, MORPHOLOGY, AND SYNTAX IN THE PETERBOROUGH CHRONICLE (§§112, 122)

Comparisons of the grammars of Old and Middle English may give the impression that the curtain came down abruptly on one period and rose equally abruptly on the next. A transitional document such as the Peterborough Chronicle, which was written at intervals between the years 1121 and 1154, shows the mixture of Old and Middle English forms that could occur on a single page. For the year 1123, vowels in unstressed syllables are often reduced to [ə], spelled *e,* but not invariably so. The noun has sometimes lost its dative singular inflectional *-e,* but it sometimes retains it. The definite article is more conservative than the noun, retaining the nominative singular *se,* the accusative singular *þone,* and the plural *þa,* instead of generalizing to the invariable *þe.* The personal pronoun plural has the OE *hi* instead of the later form in Chaucer, *they.* The syntax shows all the possibilities of Old English for subject and verb—SV, VS, SOV, and in subordinate clauses S . . . V—but the proportions appear to be shifting toward the modern invariable SV. The language, then, is neither Old English nor the late Middle English of Chaucer but a transitional variety of the first half of the twelfth century.

The text from the Peterborough Chronicle has the Modern English gloss above it and selected, normalized Old English glosses below. Put checks on the chart opposite the italicized words and phrases to show the mixture of older and newer features. Some phrases illustrate more than one feature.[8]

[8]The text is from Cecily Clark's edition, *The Peterborough Chronicle 1070–1154,* 2nd ed. (Oxford: Clarendon, 1970), pp. 42–43.

Older Features

Def. Art. = *se, þone,* and *þa* rather than the invariable *þe*
Dat. -e = retention of dative inflection on nouns after prepositions
    Ex.: *ofer eal Englalande*
Pro. *h*-forms = OE *h*-form rather than ON *th*-form
VS = Verb-Subject order in main clauses
    Ex.: *sende se kyng*
SOV = Finite verb at the end of subordinate clause

Newer Features

-e(n), -es = Reduction to -e [ə] of the full vowels e, a, o, u in unstressed syllables
    Ex.: *sona > sone*
Loss of Dat. -e = No dative inflection on nouns after prepositions
SV = This order occurred regularly in OE, but the feature that is "newer" is the increased proportion of its use, at the expense of VS, SOV, and S . . . V. Check the box whenever SV occurs.

From the Entry for 1123

	Older Features					Newer Features		
Def. Art.	Dat. -e	Pro. hi	VS	SOV	-e(n), -es	Loss of Dat. -e	SV

Soon   thereafter   sent the king   his
Ða *sone* þæræfter *sende se kyng* hise
   sona

writs   over all England   and bade
write ofer eal Englalande and bed
writ-u   Englaland-e

his   bishops   and his   abbots   and
hise *biscopes* and hise abbates and
    biscop-as

his   thegns   all   that they should
hise *þeignes* ealle þet *hi scolden*
    þegn-as   hi sceold-on

come   to his council   on Candlemass
cumen to his gewitenemot on Candelmesse
cum-an

day   at Gloucester   him   towards;   and
deig to Gleawceastre him togeanes; and
dæg-e

they so did.   When they were   there
hi swa *diden.* Ða hi wæran þær
hi   dyd-on

gathered,   then bade the king them that
gegaderod, þa *bed se kyng heom* þæt

Older Features					Newer Features		
Def. Art.	Dat. -e	Pro. hi	VS	SOV	-e(n), -es	Loss of Dat. -e	SV

they should   choose them archbishop to
hi scolden cesen hem ærcebiscop to
            ceos-an

Canterbury   whomsover   they
Cantawarabyrig swa hwam swa swa *hi*

wished   and   he them it would   grant.
woldon and *he hem hit wolde tyþian.*

Then spoke   the bishops among themselves
Ða spræcon *ða* biscopas hem betwenan

and   said   that they never   more   wished
and *sæden* þæt hi næfre mare ne wolden
        sæd-on

to have monastic   man as archbishop   over
haven munechades man to *ercebiscop* ofer
                    arcerbiscop-e

them, but went   all   together   to the
hem, ac iedon ealle samodlice to þone

king   and asked   that they might choose
kyng and ieornden þet *hi mosten cesen*
                moston ceos-an

of clerical   man whomever   they
of clerchades man swa hwam swa swa *hi*

wished   for archbishop;   and the king   it
wolden to *ercebiscop;* and *se kyng hit*
wold-on   arcebiscop-e

them granted.
hem tidde.

7.5 CHAUCER'S PRONUNCIATION

1. The results of the vowel changes described in §7.2 can be summarized for easy reference in reading Chaucer.[9]

[9]This summary is adapted from Albert C. Baugh, ed., *Chaucer's Major Poetry* (Englewood Cliffs, N.J.: Prentice-
Hall, 1963), where one can find a full discussion of open and close *e* [ɛ:], [e:] and open and close *o* [ɔ:], [o:], pp. xxiii–
xxvi.

Sound	Spelling	Example
[ɑ]	a	what
[ɑ:]	a, aa	fader, caas
[ɛ]	e	hem
[ɛ:]	e, ee	bere, heeth
[e:]	e, ee	swete, neede
[ɪ]	i, y	list, nyste
[i:]	i, y	blithe, nyce
[ɔ]	o	for
[ɔ:]	o, oo	lore, goon
[o:]	o, oo	dom, roote
[ʊ]	u, o	ful, nonne
[u:]	ou, ow	hous, how
[y]	u	vertu
[ə]	e	yonge
[ɑʊ]	au, aw	cause, drawe
[ɛɪ]	ai, ay, ei, ey	fair, may, feith, eyr
[ɛʊ]	ew	fewe, shewe
[ɪʊ]	eu, ew	reule, newe
[oʊ]	ou, ow	thought, knowe
[ɔɪ]	oi, oy	point, joye

2. Most of the consonants were pronounced in Chaucer's English as in Modern English. Consonants which have become silent in certain positions in Modern English were still pronounced:

k before **n**	knyght	[knɪxt]
g before **n**	gnawe	[gnɑʊwə]
l before **f, v, k**	calf	[kɑlf]
	halve	[hɑlvə]
	folk	[fɔlk]
w before **r**	write	[wri:tə]

The *gh* in *knyght* represents the voiceless velar fricative [x]. Initial *th* in *that, the,* etc. may have remained the voiceless fricative [θ] as in Old English, or, in more advanced dialects, may have had the modern voiced pronunciation [ð]. The *r* in Chaucer's English was trilled.

3. Perhaps the most popular and surely the most often memorized lines of English poetry from the medieval period are those of the beginning of the *General Prologue* to the *Canterbury Tales*. The feel for Chaucer's verse form and language that one gains from the exercise is well worth the amount of effort that it takes to learn these lines by heart. Memorize the first 42 lines.[10]

Whan that Aprill with his shoures soote	hwɑn θat ɑ:prɪl wɪθ hɪs šu:rəs so:tə
The droghte of March hath perced to the roote,	θə dru:xt ɔf mɑrč hɑθ pɛ:rsəd to: θə ro:tə
And bathed every veyne in swich licour	ɑnd bɑ:ðəd ɛvrɪ vɛɪn ɪn swɪč lɪku:r
Of which vertu engendred is the flour;	ɔf hwɪč vɛrty ɛnǰɛndrəd ɪs θə flu:r
Whan Zephirus eek with his sweete breeth	hwɑn zɛfɪrʊs e:k wɪθ hɪs swe:tə brɛ:θ
Inspired hath in every holt and heeth	ɪnspi:rəd hɑθ ɪn ɛvrɪ hɔlt ɑnd he:θ

5

---

[10]Quotations from Chaucer throughout are from Albert C. Baugh, ed. *op. cit.*

The tendre croppes, and the yonge sonne	θə tɛndrə krɔppəs and θə juŋɡə sunnə
Hath in the Ram his halve cours yronne,	haθ ɪn θə ram hɪs halvə kuːrs ɪrunnə
And smale foweles maken melodye,	and smaːlə fuːləs maːkən mɛlɔdiːə
That slepen al the nyght with open yë	θat sleːpən al θə nɪxt wɪθ ɔːpən iːə	10
(So priketh hem nature in hir corages),—	sɔː prɪkɛθ hɛm naːtyr ɪn hɪr kuraːjəs
Thanne longen folk to goon on prilgrimages,	θan lɔŋɡən fɔlk toː goːn ɔn pɪlɡrɪmaːjəs
And palmeres for to seken straunge strondes,	and palmɛrs fɔr toː seːkən straunjə strɔndəs
To ferne halwes, kowthe in sondry londes;	toː fɛrnə halwəs kuːθ ɪn sundrɪ londəs
And specially from every shires ende	and spɛsɪalɪ frɔm ɛvrɪ šiːrəs ɛndə	15
Of Engelond to Caunterbury they wende,	ɔf ɛŋɡəlɔnd toː kauntərbriː θɛɪ wɛndə
The hooly blisful martir for to seke,	θə hɔːlɪ blɪsful martɪr fɔr toː seːkə
That hem hath holpen whan that they were	θat hɛm haθ hɔlpən hwan θat θɛɪ weːr seːkə
seeke.	
Bilfil that in that seson on a day,	bɪfɪl θat ɪn θt sɛːzun ɔn ə dɛɪ
In Southwerk at the Tabard as I lay	ɪn suθwɛrk at θə tabard as iː lɛɪ	20
Redy to wenden on my pilgrymage	rɛdɪ toː wɛndən ɔn miː pɪlɡrɪmaːjə
To Caunterbury with ful devout corage,	toː kauntərbriː wɪθ ful deːvuːt kuraːjə
At nyght was come into that hostelrye	at nɪxt was kum ɪntoː θat hɔstɛlriːə
Wel nyne and twenty in a compaignye,	wɛl niːn and twɛntɪ ɪn ə kumpɛɪniːə
Of sondry folk, by aventure yfalle	ɔf sundrɪ fɔlk biː aːventyr ɪfallə	25
In felaweshipe, and pilgrimes were they alle,	ɪn fɛlaušip and pɪlɡrɪms weːr θɛɪ allə
That toward Caunterbury wolden ryde.	θat toːward kauntərburɪ woːldən riːdə
The chambres and the stables weren wyde,	θə čaːmbrəs and θə staːbləs weːrən wiːdə
And wel we weren esed atte beste.	and wɛl weː weːrən ɛːzəd attə bɛstə
And shortly, whan the sonne was to reste,	and šortlɪ hwan θə sunnə was toː rɛstə	30
So hadde I spoken with hem everichon	sɔː had iː spɔːkən wɪθ hɛm ɛvrɪčɔːn
That I was of hir felaweshipe anon,	θat iː was ɔf hɪr fɛlaušip anɔːn
And made forward erly for to ryse,	and maːdə fɔrward ɛːrlɪ fɔr toː riːzə
To take oure wey ther as I yow devyse.	toː taːk uːr wɛɪ θɛːr as iː juː deːviːzə
But nathelees, whil I have tyme and space,	but naːðɛlɛːs hwiːl iː hav tiːm and spaːsə	35
Er that I ferther in this tale pace,	ɛːr θat iː fɛrðər ɪn θɪs taːlə pasə
Me thynketh it acordaunt to resoun	meː θɪŋkəθ ɪt akɔrdaunt toː rɛːzuːn
To telle yow al the condicioun	toː tɛllə juː al θə kɔndɪsɪuːn
Of ech of hem, so as it semed me,	ɔf ɛːč ɔf hɛm sɔː as ɪt seːməd meː
And whiche they weren, and of what degree,	and hwɪč θɛɪ weːrən and ɔf hwat deːgreː	40
And eek in what array that they were inne;	and eːk ɪn hwat arrɛɪ θat θɛɪ weːr ɪnnə
And at a knyght than wol I first bigynne.	and at ə knɪxt θan wul iː fɪrst bɪgɪnnə

7.6 MIDDLE ENGLISH NOUNS (§113)

The declensions of Old English nouns described in §3.6 were reduced in Chaucer's language to one principal pattern, illustrated by *dom* 'judgment' and *name:*

Singular	N., D., A.	**dom**	**name**
	G.	**domes**	**names**
Plural	N., G., D., A	**domes**	**names**

The dative, nominative, and accusative have the same form in the singular and contrast with the genitive; in the plural all four cases are the same.

Exceptions

Most of the exceptions to this pattern reflect distinctions that were made in Old English. These exceptions are occasional, and for all of them there are Middle English occurrences of the new regular form as well. All the examples below are from Chaucer.

1. Genitive singular of weak nouns:

Til I myn owen *herte* blood may see *(Troilus 2.445)*
                heart's

The *-e* of *herte blood* derives from the weak declension's *-an* in the genitive singular (cf. Old English *heortan blod* 'heart's blood'). The *-n* dropped and the *a* was reduced to [ə], spelled *e*.

2. Genitive singular of nouns of relationship:

Now, by my *fader* soule that is deed (A 781)
             father's   dead

The nouns of relationship ending in *-r (father, daughter, sister, mother, brother)* often have no ending in the genitive singular (cf. Old English *fæder rice* 'father's kingdom', §3.6).

3. Genitive singular of nouns ending in *-s:*

Of *Venus* werkes worth his olde sho (D 708)
   Venus's acts   shoe

Phonetic assimilation causes the frequent loss of inflectional *-s* in words that end in *-s*.

4. Dative singular in petrified phrases:

For in this world was noon so fair *on-lyve* (H 122)
                         none   alive
       Compare, without the *-e:*

No man hateth his flessh, but in his *lyf* (E 1386)
                                      life

The dative generally has the same form as the nominative and the accusative, but the *-e* shows up in "petrified phrases" such as *on lyve* 'alive', *on fyre* 'afire', *to bedde, to shippe, with childe*.

5. Plural of weak nouns:

Up to the tree he caste his *eyen* two (E 2360)
                             eyes

By the late fourteenth century the strong ending in *-es* had become the normal inflection for the plural in all parts of England. Chaucer retains the weak ending in a few nouns such as *eyen* 'eyes', *asshen* 'ashes', *been* 'bees', *fon* 'foes', and *oxen* 'oxen'. Some of these were originally strong, and they have the weak ending by analogy. Most of them occur also with the *-s* inflection.

6. Plural of long-stem neuter nouns:

To buggen þe *sep* and *swin (anon., Dame Sirith 272)*
purchase thee sheep   swine

    These derive from long-stem neuter nouns in Old English, which had no ending in the nominative and accusative plural (cf. §3.6).

7. Umlaut plural:

So that ye *men* shul been as lewed as *gees* (E 2275)
          shall be   foolish

    Cf. Old English *mann/menn, gos/ges,* etc. (§3.6).

8. Plural of nouns ending in *-s:*

He made of ryme ten *vers* or twelve (*Book of the Duchess* 463)
                verses

    In the blank next to each sentence, indicate why the italicized noun differs from the majority of Middle English nouns by writing the number that refers to the exception listed above.

_____ 1. I hadde the prente of seinte *Venus* seel (Chaucer, D 604)
               print   holy   Venus's

_____ 2. That is thi *brother* wif, if ich it wiste (Chaucer, *Troilus* 1.678)
              brother's   I   knew

_____ 3. In termes hadde he *caas* and doomes alle (Chaucer, A 323)
           Year Books   cases   judgments

_____ 4. It tikleth me about myn *herte* roote (Chaucer, D 471)
                    heart's

_____ 5. He grynte with his *teeth,* so was he wrooth (Chaucer, D 2161)
          gnashed   angry

_____ 6. Her beþ boþe *shep* and *get* [Two nouns] (anon., *The Fox and the Wolf* 167)
          are   sheep   goats

_____ 7. Suþþe þe portereuse house hii sette *a fure* anon (anon., *Robert of*
      Then   bailiff's   they   afire
Gloucester 164)

_____ 8. And þe barons ek hor *fon* at aȝen hom armes bere (*Ibid.,* 70)
                 also their foes   against them   bore

_____ 9. That was my *lady* name ryght (Chaucer, *Duchess* 949)
             lady's

    Note: The Old English noun was weak, and the genitive singular was *hlæfdigan.*

_____ 10. þe iles of the Oryent to *Ercules* boundes (anon., *Parle. of the Thre Ages* 334)
           isles   Hercules's

_____   11. Thanne waked he of his wynkyng and wiped his *eyghen* (Langland, *Piers*

                          eyes

                 Pl. B 5.361)

_____   12. And whan he was woxen more in his *moder* absence (*Ibid.,* 19.120)

                          grown   mother's

7.7 MIDDLE ENGLISH ADJECTIVES (§114)

During the Middle English period the adjective lost all distinctions of case and gender and, in the weak declension, distinctions of number as well. The difference between the strong and weak declensions is maintained only among monosyllabic adjectives that end in a consonant, such as *yong* 'young', and among these only in the singular. Among adjectives that do not end in a consonant, such as *swete* 'sweet', and generally among adjectives of two syllables, such as *gentil* 'gentle', even this difference is lacking:

	Singular	*Plural*
Strong	**yong**	**yonge**
Weak	**yonge**	**yonge**

Invariable: **swete** (ends in a vowel), **gentil** (disyllabic)[11]
The weak declension is used:

1. When the adjective follows

    a. The definite article
    b. A demonstrative pronoun
    c. A possessive pronoun
    d. A noun in the genitive case

2. When it modifies a following noun used in direct address
3. Often when it modifies a proper noun

The strong declension is used when the adjective is unaccompanied before the noun and when it functions as a predicate adjective. (The plural of the predicate adjective sometimes has the regular *-e* ending and sometimes has no ending.)

In the following sentences from Chaucer's *Canterbury Tales* circle Strong, Weak, or Invariable for each italicized adjective. (In the last category are adjectives of more than one syllable and those ending in a vowel. Only for adjectives such as *yong* should Strong or Weak be circled.) Supply the *-e* if the inflectional ending is needed.

---

[11]Although adjectives of two syllables were generally uninflected, adjectives of three syllables often took an inflectional *-e*. This made a fourth syllable that sustained the naturally alternating rhythms of English prose and the

                                    x /   x\ x   /
pattern of the iambic pentameter: *the semelieste man.* For a full study of final *-e* in adjectives and in other contexts, and an explanation of rhythmical determinants, see Donka Minkova, *The History of Final Vowels in English: The Sound of Muting* (Berlin: Mouton de Gruyter, 1991).

1. With hym there was his sone, a *yong____* Squier (A 79)

   Strong   Weak   Invariable

2. The *yong____* girles of the diocise (A 664)

   Strong   Weak   Invariable

3. Anon he yaf the *sik____* man his boote (A 424)
   gave

   Strong   Weak   Invariable

4. This *worthy____* man ful wel his wit bisette (A 279)
   employed

   Strong   Weak   Invariable

5. A bowe he bar and arwes *bright____* and kene (A 1966)
   bore   arrows   sharp

   Strong   Weak   Invariable

6. The *open____* werre, with woundes al bibledde (A 2002)
   war   covered with blood

   Strong   Weak   Invariable

7. The *cold____* deeth, with mouth gapyng upright (A 2008)
   death   face up

   Strong   Weak   Invariable

8. For he was *wys____* and koude soone espye (A 1420)
   could

   Strong   Weak   Invariable

9. Allas, thou *fell____* Mars! allas, Juno! (A 1559)
   cruel

   Strong   Weak   Invariable

10. Whilom, as *old____* stories tellen us (A 859)
    Once upon a time

    Strong   Weak   Invariable

11. And Emelye, clothed al in *grene____* (A 1686)

    Strong   Weak   Invariable

12. Thanked be Fortune and hire *fals____* wheel (A 925)
    her

    Strong   Weak   Invariable

13. And al this voys was *sooth____*, as God is trewe (B 169)
    voice

    Strong   Weak   Invariable

14. But oon avow to *gret___* God I heete (B 334)

    one   great   promise

Strong   Weak   Invariable

15. This *fals___* knyght was slayn for his untrouthe (B 687)

Strong   Weak   Invariable

16. Hir *litel___* child lay wepyng in her arm (B 834)

Strong   Weak   Invariable

17. O *foul___* lust of luxurie, lo, thyn ende! (B 925)

Strong   Weak   Invariable

18. That in the salte see my wyf is *deed___* (B 1039)

Strong   Weak   Invariable

19. How he wol lete his *old___* sacrifices (B 325)

Strong   Weak   Invariable

20. Foryeve his *wikked___* werkes that he wroghte (B 994)

Forgive

Strong   Weak   Invariable

7.8 MIDDLE ENGLISH PERSONAL PRONOUNS (§115)

	Singular			
	First Person	Second Person	Third Person	
N.	I	thou	he	she	hit
G.	me, myn[12]	thy, thyn[12]	his	hir	his
D.	me	thee	him	hir	him
A.	me	thee	him	hir	hit

	Plural		
	First Person	Second Person	Third Person
N.	we	ye	they
G.	oure	youre	hir
D.	us	yow	hem
A.	us	yow	hem

[12]Before nouns beginning with a consonant, *my* and *thy* are used; before nouns beginning with a vowel, *myn* and *thyn*.

Study the paradigm for the personal pronoun. Pay special attention to forms that are different from modern forms. Then supply the pronouns in the following sentences from Chaucer, referring to the paradigm to check your answers. Person, number, gender, and case are provided.

1. And in _____ (*3 s m G*) gentil herte he thoughte anon (A 1772)
   immediately

2. How myghty and how greet a lord is _____ (*3 s m N*)! (A 1786)

3. And he _____ (*3 pl D*) graunteth grace, and thus he seyde (A 1828)
   grants

4. Though that _____ (*3 s f N*) were a queene or a princesse (A 1830)

5. _____ (*2 s G*) temple wol _____ (*1 s N*) worshipe everemo (A 2251)
   evermore

6. As keep me fro _____ (*2 s G*) vengeaunce and _____ (*2 s G*) ire (A 2302)

7. _____ (*1 s N*) am, _____ (*2 s N*) woost, yet of thy compaignye (A 2307)
   know

8. Now help _____ (*1 s A*), lady, sith _____ (*2 pl N*) may and kan (A 2312)
   since

9. _____ (*2 s N*) shalt ben wedded unto oon of tho (A 2351)
   one   those

10. Yif _____ (*1 s D*) the victorie, _____ (*1 s N*) aske thee namoore (A 2420)
    Give   no more

11. Gooth now _____ (*2 pl G*) way, this is the lordes wille (A 2560)

12. Whan it was day, he broghte _____ (*3 s m A*) to the halle (A 2880)

13. A brooch she baar upon _____ (*3 s f G*) lowe coler (A 3265)
    wore   collar

14. I have yfounde in _____ (*1 s G*) astrologye (A 3514)

15. And thanne shul _____ (*1 pl N*) be lordes al _____ (*1 pl G*) lyf (A 3581)

16. But certeyn, oon thyng I _____ (*2 s D*) telle (*Hous of Fame* 2002)
    one

17. "_____ (*3 s n N*) am I," quod this messager (*Duchess* 186)

18. Unto hym seyde, "Fader, why do _____ (*2 pl N*) wepe?" (B 3622)

19. For right anon _____ (*3 s f N*) wiste what _____ (*3 pl N*) mente (F 399)
    immediately   knew

20. For Goddes love, what seith _____ (*3 s n N*)? Telle it _____ (*1 pl D*)! (*Troilus* 2.96)

21. _____ (*1 pl G*) blisful Lady, Cristes mooder deere (B 1700)

22. As doon thise loveres in _____ (*3 pl G*) queynte geres (A 1531)
    moods

23. Forthi men seyn, ecch contree hath _____ (*3 s n G*) lawes (*Troilus* 2.42)
Therefore   say   each

24. Right with this swerd thanne wol _____ (*1 s N*) sle _____ (*2 pl A*) bothe (G 168)

7.9 STRONG AND WEAK VERBS IN MIDDLE ENGLISH (§§116–120)

During the fourteenth century the tendency for Old English strong verbs to become weak was at its height. The large group of weak verbs with *d* or *t* in the suffix of the preterite and past participle offered a consistent pattern of analogy for the dwindling number of strong verbs. Chaucer alternated between the strong and weak forms for the past tense and past participle in some verbs, and in others he used the older form for one principal part and the newer form for the other. Identify the verb forms from Chaucer below as strong or weak by writing S or W, respectively, in the blank provided.

_____ 1. He *walked* in the feeldes, for to prye (A 3458)
gaze

_____ 2. That in a forest faste he *welk* to wepe (*Troilus* 5.1235)
walked

_____ 3. Therwith he *weep* that pitee was to heere (A 2878)
wept

_____ 4. But soore *wepte* she if oon of hem were deed (A 148)
sorely   one   them

_____ 5. This Pompeus, this noble governour
Of Rome, which that *fleigh* at this bataille (B 3878–79)
who   fled   battle

_____ 6. He *fledde* awey for verray sorwe and shame (G 702)
true   sorrow

_____ 7. For joye him thoughte he *clawed* him on the bak (A 4326)
it seemed to him   patted

_____ 8. With that aboute y *clew* myn hed (*Hous of Fame* 3.1702)
I   scratched

_____ 9. But for the moore part they *loughe* and pleyde (A 3858)
greater   laughed   played

_____ 10. For had he *lawghed,* had he loured (*Hous of Fame* 1.409)
frowned

7.10 MIDDLE ENGLISH VERBAL INFLECTIONS (§116)

The endings for strong and weak verbs can be illustrated by *drinke(n)* 'to drink' and *hope(n)* 'to hope':

	Present Indicative	
	Strong	Weak
Sing. 1.	drink-e	hop-e
2.	drink-est	hop-est
3.	drink-eth	hop-eth
Pl.	drink-e(n)	hop-e(n)
	Present Subjunctive	
Sing.	drink-e[13]	hop-e
Pl.	drink-e(n)	hop-e(n)
	Preterite Indicative	
Sing. 1.	drank, dronk	hop-ed(e)
2.	dronk-e[13]	hop-edest
3.	drank, dronk	hop-ed(e)
Pl.	dronk-e(n)[13]	hop-ede(n), hop-ed
	Preterite Subjunctive	
Sing.	dronk-e[13]	hop-ed(e)
Pl.	dronk-e(n)[13]	hop-ede(n)
	Imperative	
Sing.	drink	hop-e
Pl.	drink-eth, drink-e	hop-eth
	Infinitive	
	drink-e(n)	hop-e(n)
	Present Participle	
	drink-ing(e)	hop-ing(e)
	Past Participle	
	dronk-e(n)[13]	hop-ed

1. Fill in the paradigms for the strong verb *synge(n)* 'to sing' and the weak verb *love(n)* 'to love'.

[13]The *o* in the second singular preterite, plural preterite, preterite subjunctive, and past participle is [ʊ].

		Present Indicative	
		Strong	Weak
Sing.	1.	_____	_____
	2.	_____	_____
	3.	_____	_____
Pl.		_____	_____

	Present Subjunctive	
Sing.	_____	_____
Pl.	_____	_____

		Preterite Indicative	
Sing.	1.	_____	_____
	2.	_____	_____
	3.	_____	_____
Pl.		_____	_____

	Preterite Subjunctive	
Sing.	_____	_____
Pl.	_____	_____

	Imperative	
Sing.	_____	_____
Pl.	_____	_____

	Present Participle	
	_____	_____

	Past Participle	
	_____	_____

2. Use the paradigm that you completed above to fill in the appropriate form of the verb in these lines from Chaucer. In each line the missing verb is a form of *syngen*. The person, number, tense, and mood are given in parentheses.

1. Wherfore I _____, (*1 s pres ind*) and synge moot certeyn (B 1853)
   sing   must   certainly

2. thou Polymya . . . _____ (*2 s pres ind*) with vois memorial in the shade
   sing   (*Anelida and Arcite* 15–18)

3. He _____ (*3 s pres ind*) in his voys gentil and smal (A 3360)
   sings

4. How that they _____ (*pl pres ind*) wel and myrily (B 4462)
   sing   merrily

5. But forth she moot, wher so she wepe or _____ (*3 s pres sub*) (B 294)
   must   whether   sing

6. And ofte tyme I _____ (*1 s pret ind*) hem loude (*Duchess* 1158)
   sang

7. Thou _____ (*2 s pret ind*) whilom lyk a nyghtyngale (H 294)
   sang   at one time

8. And after that he _____ (*3 s pret ind*) ful loude and cleere (E 1845)
   sang

9. That many a nyght they _____ (*pret pl ind*) 'weilawey!' (D 216)
   sang

10. Now _____, (*imp pl*) sire, for seinte charitee (B 4510)
    sing   holy

11. _____ (*pres par*) he was, or floytynge, al the day (A 91)
    Singing   playing the flute

12. And in his harpyng, whan that he hadde _____ (*pa par*) (A 266)
    sung

3. Complete the following lines from Chaucer with the appropriate form of the verb *love(n)*.

1. But I wol _____ (*1 s pres ind*) hire oonly and namo (A 1589)
   will love   no one else

2. "Thou _____ (*2 s pres ind*) me, I woot it wel certeyn (E 309)
   love   know

3. She _____ (*3 s pres ind*) so this hende Nicholas (A 3386)
   loves   gentle

4. I _____ (*1 s pret ind*) hire first, and tolde thee my wo (A 1146)
   loved

5. For love of hym thow _____ (*2 s pret ind*) in the shawe (*Troilus* 3.720)
   loved   grove

6. He _____ (*3 s pret ind*) so this fresshe mayden free (*Troilus* 5.1475)
   loved

7. _____ (*2 s imp*), if thee list, for I _____ (*1 s pres ind*) and ay shal (A
   Love   it pleases love   ever

   1183)

8. Of yow, which I have _____ (*pa par*) specially (B 1343)
   whom   loved

7.11 MIDDLE ENGLISH DIALECTS (§147 and Appendix A)

The boundary lines that appear on the map of Middle English dialects in Baugh and Cable §147 are oversimplified representations in several ways. The publication of *A Linguistic Atlas of Late Mediaeval English* reveals more of the complexity of the actual situation and raises basic questions about the kinds of abstractions that traditional dialectology attempts.[14] A continuum of overlapping distributions of features is a much more adequate conception than separate and clearly delineated regional dialects, although the graphic representation of such a continuum is difficult to draw and expensive to publish. The *Atlas* uses a combination of different devices: maps with dots showing the distribution of a single feature, maps with the variant linguistic items written in the locations where they occur, and "scribal profiles," or lists of features in a particular written idiolect drawn from a list of 280 features. The maps reproduced below are examples of the two major approaches to Middle English dialectology. One uses *isoglosses,* or solid lines to separate contrasting features; the other uses dots to show the mixture of usages, especially in the border areas. For the dot maps, note that all locations represented by manuscripts for the *Atlas* survey appear on each map. The half-tone shadow dots show that the form in question did not occur. The black dots show that the form did occur, and the three sizes of black dots show relative frequency of the form.[15]

1. Study the maps for *hem* and *them* and comment on the advantages of each method. (Recall that the *th-* form of the third person plural pronoun was adapted from Old Norse. It spread south replacing the native *hem* form.) Notice that for a binary opposition such as *hem-them,* one map is needed with the traditional use of isoglosses, whereas two maps are needed with dots. Why?

_____

_____

_____

_____

2. Draw your own isogloss on each of the dot maps so as to put most of the occurrences of the represented feature in the same region. Is it desirable to include *all* occurrences of the feature within the region demarcated by the isogloss? Why or why not? In what sense is an isogloss artificial?

_____

_____

_____

_____

3. If the drawing of a single isogloss is a simplification that requires disregarding some data, the grouping of "bundles of isoglosses" into dialect boundaries is even more so. The boundaries between *hem* and *them* and between *-eth* and *-es* for the third person singular present indicative are important traditional determinants of the southern boundary of the Northern dialect. Describe where the two isoglosses overlap and diverge. Compare the path of these two isoglosses with the southern boundary of the Northern dialect as shown on the map in Baugh and Cable §147. (Remember that the boundary itself is the result

---

[14]Angus McIntosh, M. L. Samuels, and Michael Benskin, *A Linguistic Atlas of Late Mediaeval English,* 4 vols. (Aberdeen: Aberdeen UP, 1986).

[15]The dot maps are from the McIntosh-Samuels-Benskin *Linguistic Atlas,* I, 314, 461, 466, and 467, reproduced by permission of Aberdeen UP. The isogloss maps are from Fernand Mossé, *A Handbook of Middle English,* trans J. A. Walker (Baltimore: Johns Hopkins UP, 1952), reproduced by permission of Johns Hopkins UP. These are Mossé's interpretations of the pioneering work done by Samuel Moore, Sanford B. Meech, and Harold Whitehall, "Middle English Dialect Characteristics and Dialect Boundaries," in *Univ. of Michigan Pubns in Lang. and Lit.,* vol. 13 (1935).

Figure 7.1

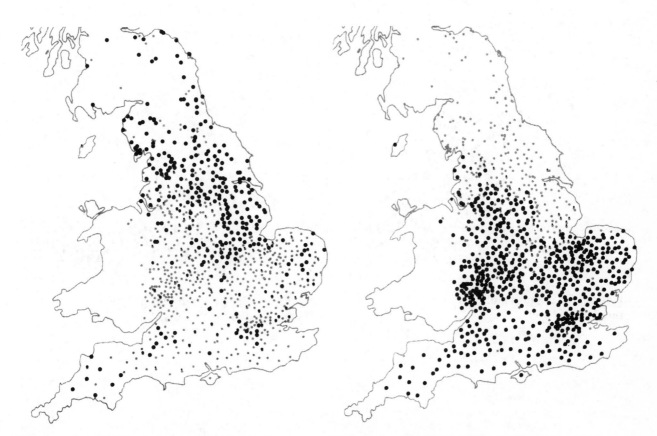

Figure 7.2   THEM: 'th-' Type, All Variants.   **Figure 7.3   THEM: 'h-' Type, All Forms.**

Figure 7.4

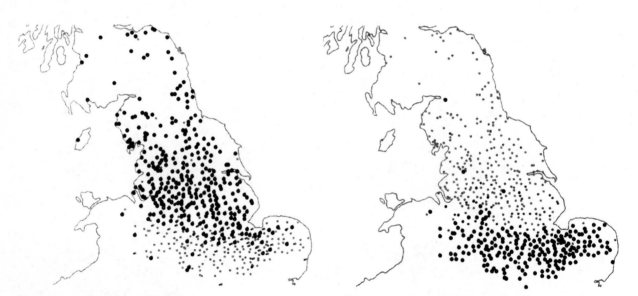

Figure 7.5 3sg pres ind: '-s' Type, Incl Abbr *-es* and *-us*.

Figure 7.6 3sg pres ind: '-th/-þ' Type (As Opposed to '-s' Type), All Variants.

of combining these two isoglosses and several others. There is no objective boundary apart from the isoglosses of which the boundary is an abstraction.)

―――――――――――――――――――――――――――――――――――――

―――――――――――――――――――――――――――――――――――――

―――――――――――――――――――――――――――――――――――――

4. The preposition *till* was adopted in Old English as *til* from Old Norse *til*. It continues to be used in some constructions alongside the native English preposition *to*. Compare the dot map for *til* below (Figure 7.7) with the map of the Danelaw on p. 50. Comment briefly on the relationship between the external, cultural history of England and the internal, linguistic history as shown by this one word. (If necessary, reread sections §68 and §77 in Baugh and Cable.)

―――――――――――――――――――――――――――――――――――――

―――――――――――――――――――――――――――――――――――――

―――――――――――――――――――――――――――――――――――――

5. Look up *dialect* in a collegiate dictionary and find the definition that comes closest to describing the variations in Middle English that are displayed here.

―――――――――――――――――――――――――――――――――――――

―――――――――――――――――――――――――――――――――――――

―――――――――――――――――――――――――――――――――――――

Figure 7.7   TO prep: 'til' Type Found in Any Context (Before C 'h' or V).

7.12 A MIDDLE ENGLISH MANUSCRIPT

An extraordinary collection of Middle English lyrics is gathered in the British Library manuscript known as Harley 2253. The beautiful lyric "Alysoun" appears in the middle of the manuscript page reproduced here. The first two stanzas and the refrain following each stanza are transcribed below. For the last two stanzas three possible transcriptions are given for each line. Put a check by the correct version. Note that one manuscript line of poetry is printed as two lines in modern editions. Line numbers refer to the manuscript, with "a" and "b" denoting first and second half-lines, respectively.

Bytuene mersh° & aueril°	March / April
When spray° biginneþ to springe°	twig / grow
þe lutel° foul° haþ hire° wyl	little / bird / her
on hyre lud° to synge	song
Ich° libbe° in louelonginge°	I / live / love-longing
for semlokest° of alle þynge	most seemly
He° may me blisse bringe	She
icham in hire baundoun°	power

[Refrain]

5	An hendy hap ichabbe yhent	A fair fortune I have received
	ichot° from heuene it is me sent	I know
	from alle wymmen mi loue is lent°	gone
	& lyht° on Alysoun	alit

On heu° hire her° is fayr ynoh	color / hair
hire browe broune hire eȝe blake	
Wiþ lossum° chere° he on me loh°	lovely / countenance / laughed
wiþ middel° smal & wel ymake°	waist / made
Bote he° me wolle to hire take	she
forte° buen° hire owen make°	for to / be / mate

10	Longe to lyuen ichulle° forsake°	I will / refuse
	& feye° fallen adoun	fated

[Refrain]

An hendy hap &c

Consult the page from the manuscript, and put a check by the correct version below:

Line 11a

Fihtes° when y bende° in bak°	fights / bent / back
Fishes then yspreynd° & wake°	scattered / weak
Nihtes when y wende° & wake	turn

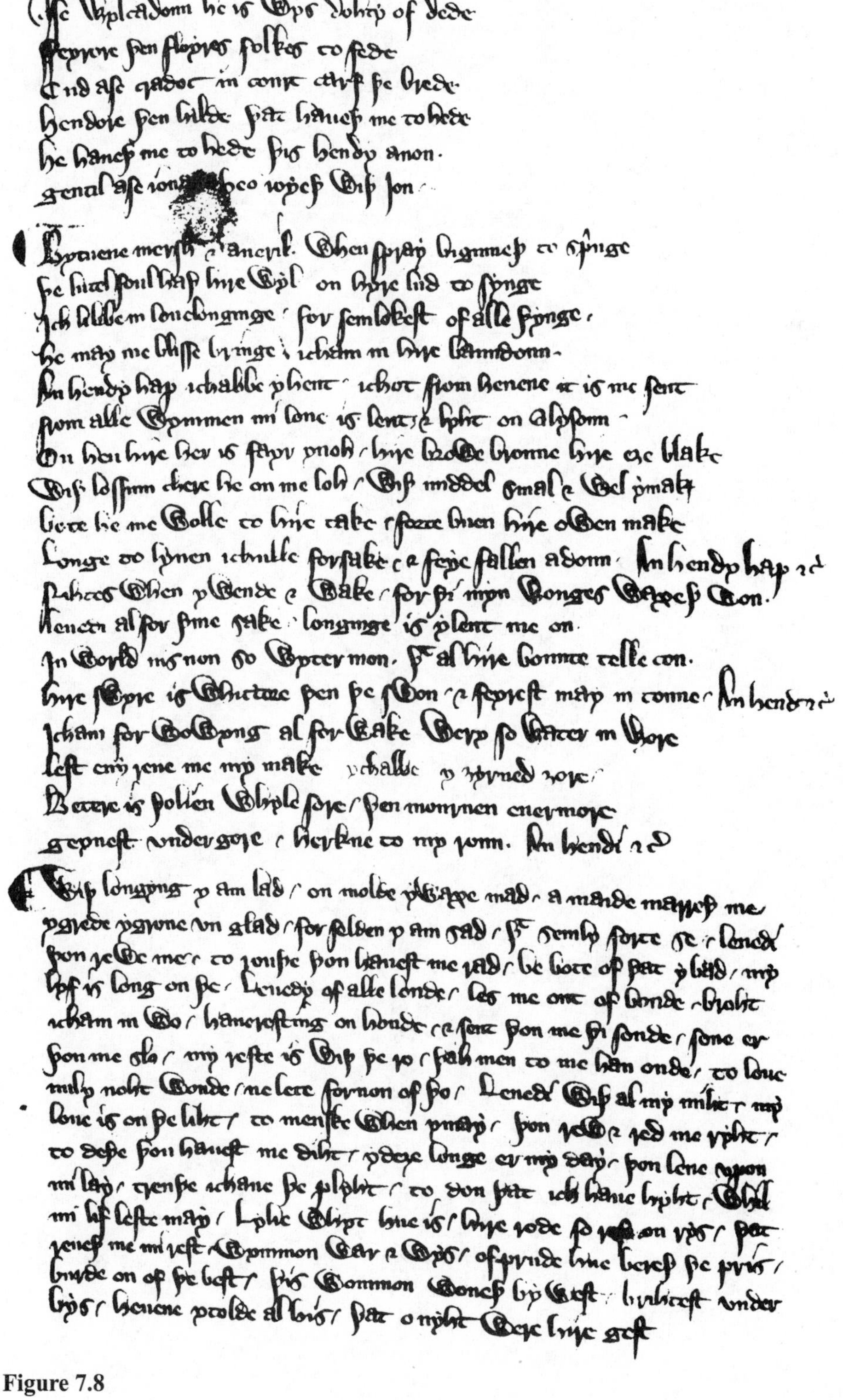

Figure 7.8

Line 11b

for þe myn wonges° wepen° won°   cheeks / weep / pallid
forþi° myn wonges waxeþ° won   therefore / grow
foule° myre° wonger° wepeþ° won   foul / mire / pillow / weeps

Line 12a

leuedi° al for þine sake   lady
lengþe° as for some rake   length
lengore° al for þine ake°   longer / ache

Line 12b

louynge° is ylent° men on   praising / arrived
langage & glent° me on   glance
longinge is ylent me on

Line 13a

In world nis non so wyter° mon   wise
In world mones° go wythinne   moons
In world mis° now so sithen° mon   wrong / since

Line 13b

þ(a)t al hire beaute telle con
þ(a)t al hire gomme° telle con   gum
þ(a)t al hire bounte° telle con   goodness

Line 14a

hire swyre° is swetture° þen þe plom°   neck / sweeter / plum
hire swyre is whittore° þen þe swon   whiter
hire swyre is stronger þen þe ston

Line 14b

& feyrest may me conne°   know
& feyrest malt in tonne°   cask
& feyrest may° in toune   maid

Refrain

An hendi &c

Line 15a

Icham° for bobbying al forwake°   I am / weary with waking
Icham for wowyng° al forwake   wooing
Icham for þrowyng al forwake

Line 15b

wery so° water in wore°   as / motion
bery° so latter° in hope   berry / later
Weve° þo° gates in hope   weave / those

Line 16a

lest eny yeue° me mor° mase°   give / me / confusion
lest eny reue° me my make°   take from / mate
lest eny renne° ine my maine°   run / strength

Line 16b

ychulle° y-ȝyrne° ȝore°   I will / yearn / for a long time
ychabbe° ierned° ore   I have / earned
ychabbe y-ȝyrned° ȝore   yearned

Line 17a

Betere is folwen° whale fore°   to follow / beforehand
Betere is þolien° whyle° sore°   to suffer / a while / sorely
Betere is flowen° whyle fore   to flow

Line 17b

þen° mournen euermore   than
þen morwe° euermore   morrow
þen moeven° euermore   move

Line 18a

geynest° vnder gore°   handsomest / clothing
geynest undergrowe°   of short stature
greyest vndergone

Line 18b

herkne° to my nome   listen
herkne to my roun°   song
herte° to my soun°   heart / sound

Refrain

An hendi &c.

7.13 THE LANGUAGE ILLUSTRATED[16]

The Wycliffe Bible

The first complete translation of the Bible into English was inspired by the Oxford reform leader, John Wycliffe, about 1380–83. Although it is known as the Wycliffe Bible, the extent of Wycliffe's actual contribution to the project is uncertain. After the first translation from the Latin Vulgate, a revised version in a simpler style, generally attibuted to John Purvey, was completed about 1395. The revised version is the one from which the following two selections are taken.[17]

Moses and the Red Sea
Exodus 14.21–31

And whanne Moises hadde stretchid forth the hond on the see, the Lord took it awei,

the while a greet wynde and brennynge blew in al the niȝt, and turnede in to dryenesse;
burning

and the watir was departid. And the sones of Israel entriden by the myddis of the drye
entered

see; for the watir was as a wal at the riȝt side and left side of hem. And Egipcians

pursueden, and entriden aftir hem, al the ridyng of Farao, hise charis, and knyȝtis, bi the
entered   procession   chariots

myddis of the see. And the wakyng of the morewtid cam thanne, and lo! the Lord
morning

bihelde on the castels of Egipcians, bi a piler of fier, and of cloude, and killide the oost
encampment   pillar   host

of hem; and he destriede the wheelis of charis, and tho weren borun in to the depthe.
those

Therefor Egipcians seiden, Fle we Israel; for the Lord fiȝtith for hem aȝenus vs. And the

Lord seide to Moises, Holde forth thin hond on the see, that the watris turne aȝen to

Egipicians, on the charis, and knyȝtis of hem. And whanne Moises hadde hold forth the
chariots

hoond aȝens the see, it turnede aȝen first in the morewtid to the formere place; and
morning

whanne Egipcians fledden, the watris camen aȝen, and the Lord wlappide hem in the
enveloped

[16]For examples of the Northern, Southern, and Kentish dialects and additional examples of East Midland and West Midland, with comments, see Baugh and Cable, Appendix A.

[17]From Josiah Forshall and Frederic Madden, eds., *The Holy Bible . . . Made from the Latin Vulgate by John Wycliffe and his Followers* (Oxford: Oxford University Press, 1850), I, 225–26.

myddis of the floodis. And the watris turneden aȝen, and hiliden the charis, and knyȝtis
covered

of al the oost of Farao, which sueden, and entriden in to the see; sotheli not oon of hem
host   entered   verily   one

was alyue. Forsothe the sones of Israel ȝeden thorouȝ the myddis of the drye see, and
guided

the watris weren to hem as for a wal, on the riȝt side and left side. And in that dai the

Lord delyuerede Israel fro the hond of Egipcians, and thei sien Egipcians deed on the
saw   dead

brynke of the see, and thei seiȝen the greet hond which the Lord hadde vsid aȝens hem;

and the puple dredde the Lord, and thei bileueden to the Lord, and to Moises his
feared   believed

seruaunt.

The Nativity[18]
Luke 2.1–14

And it was don in tho daies, a maundement wente out fro the emperour August, that
those   decree

al the world schulde be discryued. This firste discryuyng was maad of Cyryn, iustice of
enumerated   census   by Cyrenius

Sirie. And alle men wenten to make professioun, ech in to his owne citee. And Joseph
Syria

wente vp fro Galilee, fro the citee Nazareth, in to Judee, in to a citee of Dauid, that is

clepid Bethleem, for that he was of the hous and of the meyne of Dauid, that he schulde
named   family

knouleche with Marie, his wijf, that was weddid to hym, and was greet with child. And
register

it was don, while thei weren there, the daies were fulfillid, that sche schulde bere child.

And sche bare hir first borun sone, and wlappide hym in clothis, and leide hym in a
wrapped

cratche, for ther was no place to hym in no chaumbir. And scheepherdis weren in the
manger

same cuntre, wakynge and kepynge the watchis of the nyȝt on her flok. And lo! the

aungel of the Lord stood bisidis hem, and the cleernesse of God schinede aboute hem;

and thei dredden with greet drede. And the aungel seide to hem, Nyle ȝe drede; for lo!
were afraid   fear   Do not ye fear

Y preche to ȝou a greet ioye, that schal be to al puple. For a sauyoure is borun to dai to

[18]*Ibid.*, IV, 148–49.

ȝou, that is Crist the Lord, in the citee of Dauid. And this is a tokene to ȝou; ȝe schulen

fynde a ȝong child wlappid in clothis, and leid in a cratche. And sudenli ther was maad

wrapped   manger

with the aungel a multitude of heuenli knyȝthod, heriynge God, and seiynge, Glorie be

praising

in the hiȝeste thingis to God, and in erthe pees be to men of good wille.

Chaucer

For an example of London English durign the late fourteenth century Chaucer has with good reason been the perennial standard. His composition of the *Canterbury Tales* was probably undertaken between the years 1387 and 1395—the *General Prologue* at the beginning of that period, the *Nun's Priest's Tale* more likely near the end. The most important difference to be aware of between Chaucer's English and ordinary London speech is in the final -*e*. Chaucer's use of the inflectional syllable for metrical purposes is a conservative feature of his poetic language, which the speech of his day had almost certainly lost.

From The Nun's Priest's Tale[19]

Heere bigynneth the Nonnes Preestes Tale of the Cok and Hen, Chauntecleer and Pertelote.

A povre wydwe, somdeel stape in age

poor   widow   somewhat advanced

Was whilom dwellying in a narwe cotage,

     once upon a time   small

Biside a grove, stondynge in a dale.

This wydwe, of which I telle yow my tale,

Syn thilke day that she was last a wyf,   4015

Since the same

In pacience ladde a ful symple lyf,

    patience   led

For litel was hir catel and hir rente.

               possessions   income

By housbondrie of swich as God hire sente

             such

She foond hirself and eek hir doghtren two.

          also   daughters

Thre large sowes hadde she, and namo,   4020

       no more

[19]From Albert C. Baugh, ed., *op. cit.*

Three keen, and eek a sheep that highte Malle.
kine   was named
(cows)

Ful sooty was hir bour and eek hir halle,
                    bower   hall

In which she eet ful many a sklendre meel.
                ate   slender

Of poynaunt sauce hir neded never a deel.
    piquant   (for) her was necessary   bit

No deyntee morsel passed thurgh hir throte;   4025
    dainty

Hir diete was accordant to hir cote.
                in harmony with   cottage

Repleccioun ne made hire nevere sik;
Repletion

Attempree diete was al hir phisik,
    Temperate   medicine

And exercise, and hertes suffisaunce.
                    content

The goute lette hire nothyng for to daunce,   4030
    hindered   not at all

N'apoplexie shente nat hir heed.
            injured

No wyn ne drank she, neither whit ne reed;

Hir bord was served moost with whit and blak,—

Milk and broun breed, in which she foond no lak,

Seynd bacoun, and somtyme an ey or tweye;   4035
Singed   egg   two

For she was, as it were, a maner deye.
                        manor dairywoman

A yeerd she hadde, enclosed al aboute

With stikkes, and a drye dych withoute,

In which she hadde a cok, hight Chauntecleer.
                    called

In al the land, of crowyng nas his peer.   4040
                    was not

His voys was murier than the murie orgon
            merrier   merry organ (singular)

On messe-dayes that in the chirche gon.
    mass days   go (pl)

Wel sikerer was his crowyng in his logge
   more careful   lodge

Than is a clokke or an abbey orlogge.
                   clock

By nature he knew ech ascencioun   4045

Of the equynoxial in thilke toun;
    equinoctial   this same

For whan degrees fiftene were ascended,

Thanne crew he, that it myghte nat been amended.
     crowed   improved upon

His coomb was redder than the fyn coral,

And batailled as it were a castel wal;   4050
    crenelated as if

His byle was blak, and as the jeet it shoon;
  bill   jet

Lyk asure were his legges and his toon;
   lapis lazuli   toes

His nayles whitter than the lylye flour,

And lyk the burned gold was his colour.
      burnished

This gentil cok hadde in his governaunce   4055

Sevene hennes for to doon al his plesaunce,
                pleasure

Whiche were his sustres and his paramours,
       sisters

And wonder lyk to hym, as of colours:
  wonderfully   in respect to

Of whiche the faireste hewed on hir throte
          colored

Was cleped faire damoysele Pertelote.   4060
  called   damsel

Curteys she was, discreet, and debonaire,
Courteous

And compaignable, and bar hyrself so faire,
  sociable   bore

Syn thilke day that she was seven nyght oold,
Since the same

That trewely she hath the herte in hoold
              her keeping

Of Chauntecleer, loken in every lith;   4065
    locked   limb

He loved hire so that wel was hym therwith.

But swich a joye was it to here hem synge,

Whan that the brighte sonne gan to sprynge,

In sweete accord, "My lief is faren in londe!"
                sweethearte gone away the country

For thilke tyme, as I have understonde,   4070
    that same

Beestes and briddes koude speke and synge.
      birds

Sir Gawain and the Green Knight

The finest Arthurian romance in English affords a good comparison with Chaucer in both its dialect and its verse form. We cannot be certain about either the time or place of composition, but there are good reasons for dating the poem about 1375 in the Northwest Midlands, possibly in Cheshire. For characteristics of the West Midland dialect, see Baugh and Cable, Appendix A, pp. 414–15.[20]

At þe fyrst quethe of þe quest quaked þe wylde;   1150
        sound   cry of   trembled   wild
                hounds   animals

Der drof in þe dale, doted for drede,
Deer rushed   valley frenzied   fear

Hiȝed to þe hyȝe, bot heterly þay were
Hurried   high   but suddenly
          ground

Restayed with þe stablye, þat stoutly ascryed.
Turned back by   ring of   loudly   shouted
            beaters

þay let þe herttez haf þe gate, with þe hyȝe hedes,
They   stags   pass by   high

þe breme bukkez also with hor brode paumez;   1155
    stout   bucks   their   antlers

For þe fre lorde hade defende in fermysoun tyme
      noble   forbidden   close-season

þat þer schulde no mon meue to þe male dere.
              interfere with

þe hindez were halden in with hay! and war!
   hinds   restrained   ware

[20]Reprinted by permission of the Oxford University Press from J. R. R. Tolkien and E. V. Gordon, eds., *Sir Gawain and the Green Knight,* 2nd ed. rev. by Norman Davis (Oxford, 1968).

þe does dryuen with gret dyn to þe depe sladez;
   (were) driven by   noise   valleys

þer myȝt mon se, as þay slypte, slentyng of arwes—   1160
   might one   see   were loosed   slanting
                                  flight

At vche wende vnder wande wapped a flone—
   each turning in the woods   swished   arrow

þat bigly bote on þe broun with ful brode hedez.
   deeply bit   in   brown hide   broad heads

What! þay brayen, and bleden, bi bonkkez þay deȝen,
        bray   bleed   on hillsides   die

And ay rachches in a res radly hem folȝes,
   always hounds   rush swiftly   follow

Hunterez wyth hyȝe horne hasted hem after   1165
          loud   hastened

Wyth such a cakkande kry as klyffes haden brusten.
        ringing   as if cliffs   had   burst

What wylde so atwaped wyȝes þat schotten
whatever animal   escaped   men   shot

Watz al toraced and rent at þe resayt,
Was   pulled slaughtered   receiving
       down   stands

Bi þay were tened at þe hyȝe and taysed to þe wattrez;
When   harassed on   high   driven   streams
                   ground

þe ledez were so lerned at þe loȝe trysteres,   1170
   men   skillful   low hunting stands

And þe grehoundez so grete, þat geten hem bylyue
     greyhounds   large   seized   quickly

And hem tofylched, as fast as frekez myȝt loke,
     pulled down   men   might look

      þer-ryȝt.
      at once

   þe lorde for blys abloy
       with joy carried
               away

   Ful oft con launce and lyȝt,   1175
   Very   did gallop   dismount

   And drof þat day wyth joy
      passed

   Thus to þe derk nyȝt.
      dark night

þus laykez þis lorde by lynde-wodez euez,
    plays   woods'   edge

And Gawayn þe god mon in gay bed lygez,
                            fair   lies

Lurkkez quyl þe daylyȝt lemed on þe wowes,   1180
Lies snug while   shone   walls

Vnder couertour ful clere, cortyned aboute;
    coverlet   bright   curtained

And as in slomeryng he slode, sleȝly he herde
          slumber   drifted subtly   heard

A littel dyn at his dor, and dernly vpon;
       noise   stealthily open

And he heuez vp his hed out of þe cloþes,
      lifts   bedclothes

A corner of þe cortyn he caȝt vp a lyttel,
              curtain   raised

And waytez warly þiderwarde quat hit be myȝt.   1186
    looked   warily in that   what   might
                 direction

Hit watz þe ladi, loflyest to beholde,
    was   loveliest

þat droȝ þe dor after hir ful dernly and stylle,
    closed   very stealthily   quietly

And boȝed towarde þe bed; and þe burne schamed,
    turned   knight was embarrassed

And layde hym doun lystyly, and let as he slepte;   1190
              artfully   pretended that

And ho stepped stilly and stel to his bedde,
    she   softly   stole

Kest vp þe cortyn and creped withinne,
Cast

And set hir ful softly on þe bed-syde,
      seated herself

And lenged þere selly longe to loke quen he wakened.
    stayed   very   see   when

þe lede lay lurked a ful longe quyle,   1195
    knight   lurking   while

Compast in his conscience to quat þat cace myȝt
Pondered   what   circumstance might

Meue oþer amount—to meruayle hym þoȝt,
Result   amount   marvelous (to) him (it) seemed
 in   to

Bot ȝet he sayde in hymself, 'More semly hit were
    yet   seemly

To aspye wyth my spelle in space quat ho wolde.'
  discover   speech straightway what   she wished

Þen he wakenede, and wroth, and to hir warde torned,   1200
                           stretched   toward her   turned
                           (writhed)

And vnlouked his yȝe-lyddez, and let as hym wondered,
      opened   pretended that (it) surprised him

And sayned hym, as bi his saȝe þe sauer to worthe,
  crossed himself as if   by prayer the safer to become

     with hande.

   Wyth chynne and cheke ful swete,   1205

   Boþe quit and red in blande,
      white   mingled together

  Ful lufly con ho lete
    amiably did she speak

  Wyth lyppez smal laȝande.
    lips slender laughing

8

The Renaissance, 1500–1650

8.1 QUESTIONS FOR REVIEW

1. Explain why the following people are important in historical discussions of the English language:

Richard Mulcaster
John Hart
William Bullokar
Sir John Cheke
Thomas Wilson
Sir Thomas Elyot
Sir Thomas More
Edmund Spenser
Robert Cawdrey
Nathaniel Bailey

2. Define:

Inkhorn terms
Oversea language
Chaucerisms
Latin influence of the Fourth Period
Great Vowel Shift
His-genitive
Group possessive
Orthography

3. What new forces began to affect the English language in the Modern English period? Why may it be said that these forces were both radical and conservative?

4. What problems did the modern European languages face in the sixteenth century?

5. Why did English have to be defended as a language of scholarship? How did the scholarly recognition of English come about?

6. Who were among the defenders of borrowing foreign words?

7. What was the general attitude toward inkhorn terms by the end of Elizabeth's reign?

8. What were some of the ways in which Latin words changed their form as they entered the English language?

9. Why were some words in Renaissance English rejected while others survived?

10. What classes of strange words did sixteenth-century purists object to?

11. When was the first English dictionary published? What was the main purpose of English dictionaries throughout the seventeenth century?

12. From the discussions in Baugh and Cable §177 and below, summarize the principal features in which Shakespeare's pronunciation differs from your own.

13. Why is vowel length important in discussing sound changes in the history of the English language?

14. Why is the Great Vowel Shift responsible for the anomalous use of the vowel symbols in English spelling?

15. How does the spelling of unstressed syllables in English fail to represent accurately the pronunciation?

16. What nouns with the old weak plural in -*n* can be found in Shakespeare?

17. Why do Modern English nouns have an apostrophe in the possessive?

18. When did the group possessive become common in England?

19. How did Shakespeare's usage in adjectives differ from current usage?

20. What distinctions, at different periods, were made by the forms *thou, thy, thee*? When did the forms fall out of general use?

21. How consistently were the nominative *ye* and the objective *you* distinguished during the Renaissance?

22. What is the origin of the form *its*?

23. When did *who* begin to be used as a relative pronoun? What are the sources of the form?

24. What forms for the the third person singular of the verb does one find in Shakespeare? What happened to these forms during the seventeenth century?

25. How would cultivated speakers of Elizabethan times have regarded Shakespeare's use of the double negative in "Thou hast spoken no word all this time—nor understood none neither"?

8.2 DICTIONARIES OF HARD WORDS (§170)

More than most traditions of the humanities, English lexicography during its first century and a half build steadily and progressively on preceding works. Each dictionary maker copied from predecessors in ways that were sometime blatant, sometimes disguised, but usually more excusable than an equivalent amount of literary plagiarism would be.[1] Even the first English dictionary, Robert Cawdrey's *A Table Alphabeticall of Hard Words* (1604), had its direct sources. Though Cawdrey had no English dictionary to copy from, he did have tables of hard words with brief definitions in the schoolbooks of the sixteenth century, especially Edmund Coote's *The English School Master* (1596). He also had Latin-English dictionaries in which he could find the original forms of the English "hard words" together with definitions in English; Cawdrey drew heavily on the 1596 edition of Thomas Thomas's Latin-English dictionary, and subsequent English lexicographers drew on later editions.

Definitions from the first six English dictionaries and two of their predecessors, Coote's schoolbook and Thomas's Latin-English dictionary, are listed after the chart below. In the

---

[1] See De Witt T. Starnes and Gertrude E. Noyes, *The English Dictionary from Cawdrey to Johnson, 1604–1755* (Chapel Hill: University of North Carolina Press, 1946); rpt. with new introduction and bibliography by Gabriele Stein (Amsterdam: Benjamins, 1991).

chart, identify the one or two most likely sources for the definition of each word in each dictionary. If several dictionaries have the same definition and it is impossible to name the immediate source, list the two chronologically closest ones and "etc."

	Degenerate	Fabulous	Graduate	Ostracism	Prostitute	Sacrilege
Cawdrey	Coote Thomas					
Bullokar						
Cockeram						
Blount						
Phillips						
Coles						

degenerate

EDMUND COOTE, *The English Schoole Master* (1596): *degenerate* bee vnlike his ancestours.

THOMAS THOMAS, *Dictionarium Linguae Latinae et Anglicanae* (1596): *degener* . . . That doeth dishonestly to his stocke: in manners unlike his auncestours: base of linage, unnoble, nothing noble and courageous: growing out of kind: degenerating, faint, fearefull . . .

ROBERT CAWDREY, *A Table Alphabeticall . . . of hard usuall English words* (1604): *degenerate,* be vnlike his auncestours: to grow out of kind.

JOHN BULLOKAR, *An English Expositor* (1616): *degenerate.* To turne out of kind.

HENRY COCKERAM, *The English Dictionarie* (1623): *degenerate.* To turne out of kind.

THOMAS BLOUNT, *Glossographia* (1656): *degenerate (degenero)* to grow out of kind, to grow base.

EDWARD PHILLIPS, *The New World of English Words* (1658): *degenerate,* (lat.) to fall from a more noble to a baser kinde, to go aside from the vertues of ones Ancestors.

ELISHA COLES, *An English Dictionary* (1676): *degenerate, l.* fall from the (better) kind, from vertue, to vice, &c.

fabulous

COOTE: *fabulous* feigned.

THOMAS: *fabulosus* . . . Much talked of, that every man speaketh of, that whereof many things be fained.

CAWDREY: *fabulous,* fained, counterfeited, much talked of.

BULLOKAR: *fabulous.* False as a fable.

COCKERAM: *fabulous.* False as a lie.

BLOUNT: *fabulous (fabulosus)* full of lyes or fables.

PHILLIPS: *fabulous,* (lat.) full of Fables, or invented Tales.

COLES: *fabulous,* full of
   fables, l. invented tales.

graduate

COOTE: *graduate* that hath taken degree.
THOMAS: —
CAWDREY: *graduate,* that hath taken a degree.
BULLOKAR: *graduate.* He that hath taken a degree of learning in a publike Vniuersity.
COCKERAM: *graduate.* He that hath taken a degree of learning in a publicke University.
BLOUNT: *graduate (graduatus)* he that hath taken degree of learning in a publick University.
PHILLIPS: *graduate,* (lat.) he that hath taken a degree at the University.
COLES: *graduate, l.* having his degree.

ostracism

COOTE: —
THOMAS: *ostracismus* . . . A kind of banishment among the Athenians for ten yeres space, which was done by delivering of shels with the names of the persons condemned written in them. It was used not so much to punish other offences, as to abate the immoderate power of noble men.
CAWDREY: —
BULLOKAR: *ostracisme.* A banishment among the Athenians for ten yeares, so called because they vsed to write the names of the party so condemned, in Oyster shelles. This punishment was cheefely vsed, to abate the ouergreat power of noble men.
COCKERAM: —
BLOUNT: *ostracism (ostracismus)* a kind of banishment among the Athenians for ten years space, which was done by delivering shels with the condemned persons names written in them; It was used not so much to punish other offences, as to abate the immoderate power of Noblemen. *Tho*[*mas*].
PHILLIPS: *ostracisme,* (Greek) a kind of punishment among the *Athenians* which was a banishing for ten years by delivering shells to the condemned persons, wherein their names were written.
COLES: *ostracism,* an Athenian Banishment for ten years (by delivering a shell with the Name) *devised* by *Clisthenes,* who was the first so Condemned.

prostitute

Coote, Cawdrey, Bullokar, Cockeram, and Coles have the verb only; Blount has only the noun; Phillips has only *prostitution.*
COOTE: *prostitute* set open for vncleanenesse.
THOMAS: *prostituto* . . . To set open to euery man that commeth, to play the common bawd, or whore, to practise bawdrie and harlotrie: to abandon to euery mans abusing to get money by.
    prostituta . . . Shee that for money suffereth her selfe to be abused of all that come: a common harlot.
CAWDREY: *prostitute,* set open for vncleanesse, to set foorth to sale.
BULLOKAR: *prostitute,* to set to open sale: to offer to euery man for money.
COCKERAM: *prostitute.* To set to open sale, to offer ones bodie to every man for money.

BLOUNT: *prostitute (prostituta)* she that for money suffers her self to be abused by all that come, a common Harlot.

PHILLIPS: *prostitution,* (lat.) a Harlots letting out the use of her body for hire.

COLES: *prostitute, l.* to let out the use of her body.

sacrilege

COOTE: *sacriledge* Church-robbing.

THOMAS: *sacrilegium* . . . sacriledge, theft or taking of things out of a Church or an holy or consecrated place: also any hainous or detestable offence.

CAWDREY: *sacriledge,* church robbing, the stealing of holy things.

BULLOKAR: *sacriledge.* The robbing of a Church: the stealing of holy things, or abusing of Sacraments or holy mysteries.

COCKERAM: *sacriledge.* The robbing of a Church, the stealing of holy things, abusing of Sacraments or holy Mysteries.

BLOUNT: *sacrilege (sacrilegium)* the robbing of a Church, or other holy consecrated place, the stealing of holy things, or abusing Sacraments or holy Mysteries.

PHILLIPS: *sacrilegious,* (lat.) committing Sacriledge, *i.* a robbing of Churches, or violation of holy things.

COLES: *sacrilege, l.* the robbing of God, a Church, &c.

8.3 SHAKESPEARE'S PRONUNCIATION (§173)

Below is a phonetic transcription of lines by Shakespeare as he might have spoken them. Following the transcription is a list of some of the main differences between Shakespeare's pronunciation and the pronunciation of present-day American English. Find at least one word from the transcribed lines to illustrate each feature and enter it in the accompanying blank.

Sonnet XI

As fast as thou shalt wane so fast thou grow'st,
In one of thine, from that which thou departest,
And that fresh bloud which yongly thou bestow'st,
Thou maist call thine, when thou from youth conuertest,
Herein liues wisdome, beauty, and increase,
Without this follie, age, and could decay,
If all were minded so, the times should cease,
And threescoore yeare would make the world away:
Let those whom nature hath not made for store,
Harsh, featurelesse, and rude, barrenly perrish,
Looke whom she best indow'd, she gaue the more;
Which bountious guift thou shouldst in bounty cherrish,
  She caru'd thee for her seale, and ment thereby,
  Thou shouldst print more, not let that coppy die.

əz fæst əz ðəu šælt wɛːn soː fæst ðəu groːst
ɪn oːn əv ðəɪn frɒm ðæt hwɪč ðəu dɪpɑrtest
ən(d) ðæt freš blʊd hwɪč jʊŋlɪ ðəu bɪstoːst
ðəu mɛːst kɔl ðəɪn hwen ðəu frɒm juːθ kənvɑrtest
herɪn lɪvz wizdəm bɪuːtɪ ən(d) ɪnkrɛːs
wɪθəut ðɪs fɒlɪ ɛːj ən(d) koːld dɪkɛː
ɪf ɔːl wɛːr məɪndɪd soː ðə təɪmz šʊd sɛːs
ən(d) θriːskoːr jɛːr wʊd mɛːk ðə wərld əwɛː
let ðoːz huːm nɛːčər hæθ nɒt mɛːd fɔr stoːr
hɑrš fɛːčərles ən(d) ruːd bærənlɪ perɪš
lʊk huːm ši: best endəud ši: gɛːv ðə moːr
hwɪč bəuntjəs gift ðəu šʊdst ɪn bəuntɪ čerɪš
ši: kɑːrvd ðiː fər hər sɛːl ən(d) ment ðerbəɪ
ðəu šʊdst prɪnt moːr nɒt let ðæt kɑpɪ dəɪ

The Rape of Lucrece, Lines 1114–20

Tis double death to drowne in ken of shore,   tiz dəbəl dɛθ tʊ drəʊn ɪn kɛn əv šo:r

He ten times pines, that pines beholding food,   hi: tɛn təɪmz pəɪnz ðæt pəɪnz bɪho:ldɪŋ fu:d

To see the salue doth make the wounde ake more: tu: si: ðə sæ:v dəθ mɛ:k ðə wəʊnd ɛ:k mo:r

Great griefe greeues most at that wold do it good;   grɛ:t gri:f gri:vz mo:st æt ðæt wʊd du: ɪt gʊd

Deepe woes roll forward like a gentle flood,   di:p wo:z ro:l fɔrwərd ləɪk ə ǰɛntəl flʊd

  VVho being stopt, the bounding banks oreflowes,   hu: bi:ɪŋ stɒpt ðə bəʊndɪŋ bɛŋks o:rflo:z

Griefe dallied with nor law, nor limit knowes.   gri:f dalɪd wɪθ nɔ:r lɔ: nɔ:r limɪt no:z

1. ME *ī* [i:] was diphthongized to [əɪ], an intermediate stage in its progress to present-day [ɑɪ]: *bite* [bəɪt]. This sound and the next one can be heard in the current speech of Virginia and Canada. Examples from Shakespeare:

_____

_____

2. Similarly, the diphthongization of ME *ū* [u:] had reached [əʊ] in its progress to [ɑʊ]: *out* [əʊt]. Examples: _____

_____

_____

3. ME *ę̄* [ɛ:], which occurs in many words currently spelled with *ea*, had not yet shifted in Standard English to present-day [i]. It occurred both as the close *ę* [e:] (*sea* [se:], in the example in Baugh and Cable §173) and also, probably more commonly, still as the open *ę* sound of Middle English: *speak* [spɛ:k]. Examples:

_____

_____

4. Words from ME *ā (name)* and *ai, ay* (*dai* 'day') sometimes rhymed with words from ME *ę* (#3 above). Although there is no certainty about these sounds, at least one of their Shakespearian pronunciations must been been [ɛ:], in contrast with present-day [e:]: *face* [fɛ:s], *play* [plɛ:]. Examples: _____

_____

_____

5. The present-day reflexes of ME *ō* are [u], [ʊ], or [ə], as in *mood, stood,* and *flood.* Shakespeare rhymed these and similar words with each other, and yet we know from independent evidence that the process of shortening which led to the differentiations was taking place well before Shakespeare's time. Therefore, we do not know whether his rhymes reflect his own pronunciation or are purely traditional. Examples: _____

_____

6. In Shakespeare's English a number of words from ME *ěr,* which are now pronounced [ər] in General American, were pronounced [ɑr]: *desert* [dɛzɑrt]. Examples: _____

_____

_____

8.4 THE GREAT VOWEL SHIFT (§177)

The simple long vowels of Chaucer's Middle English patterned as we have seen:

Middle English Long Vowels

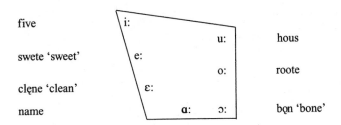

According to the series of changes known as the Great Vowel Shift, these long vowels shifted once, twice, or three times, depending on their point of origin. For certain of these shifts, front and back vowels can be grouped in pairs:

1. five [fiːvə] > [fəɪv] > [fɑɪv]
   hous [huːs] > [həʊs] > [hɑʊs]
2. swete [sweːtə] > [swiːt]
   roote [roːtə] > [ruːt]
3. name [nɑːme] > [næːm] > [nɛːm] > [neːm]
4. clẹne [klɛːnə] > [kleːn] > [kliːn]
   bọn [bɔːn] > [boːn]

Display this information on vowel trapezoids by writing in the new vowel, or pair of vowels, at each successive stage. Dotted lines represent long vowels of the previous stage. Leave them blank. Words containing the shifted vowels are given in modern spelling.

1.

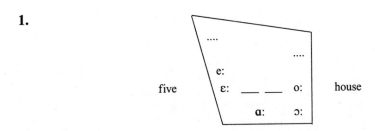

2.

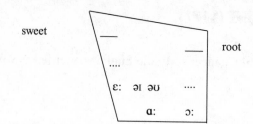

3.

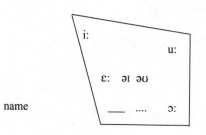

4.

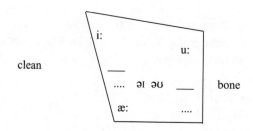

5.

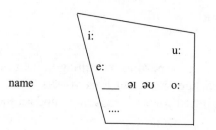

6.

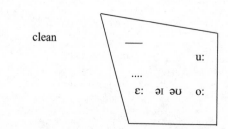

7.

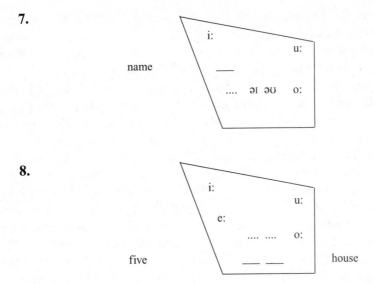

name

8.

five   house

Both the details of the Great Vowel Shift and the principles of phonological change underlying it are subjects of debate among philologists. Some authorities would present a rather different description from this one, especially in the development of ME [ɛ:], [i:], and [u:].[2]

Because the vowel shift was proceeding at different rates in different parts of the country and more quickly among the lower social classes, it is difficult to attach dates to the numbered changes. Even the relative chronology of some of the changes is questionable because of uncertainties in the evidence. Some sequences can be established clearly enough, however, because of distinctions that have been lost or retained since Middle English. ME [i:] and [u:], for example, would have been diphthongized before ME [e:] and [o:] shifted to [i:] and [u:] or else the distinction between the vowels in words like *five* and *sweet,* or *house* and *root,* would now be lost. The trapezoids in (2) and (6) show that words with ME [ɛ:], such as *clean,* shifted to [i:] *after* words with ME [e:], such as *sweet,* and thus these words preserved the historical distinction between their vowels during the early stages of the Great Vowel Shift. The paths of the mid and low front vowels are somewhat controversial because they indicate that words such as *clean,* with a vowel from ME [ɛ:], and *name,* with a vowel from ME [ɑ:], were always kept distinct.[3] However, there is some evidence from rhymes, puns, occasional spellings, and the writings of orthoepists that the distinction in the vowels of these words was lost around 1600, in some dialects at least, and then somehow reformed again later. This is a classic problem of English phonology, which raises the question of how mergers of sounds, once completed, can be undone. One explanation is that the shift of ME [ɛ:] from [e:] to [i:] in words such as *clean* was not a normal, general sound change, but the result of influence from another dialect in

[2]The present description generally follows E. J. Dobson, *English Pronunciation,* 2 vols. (Oxford: Clarendon Press, 1968), except in the treatment of ME [ɛ:]. See footnote 4, below. For problems in this traditional idealization and an argument that the vowel shift is not a history of raising but rather a history of mergers, see Robert P. Stockwell and Donka Minkova, "The English Vowel Shift: Problems of Coherence and Explanation," in *Luick Revisited,* ed. Dieter Kastovsky and Gero Bauer (Tübingen: Gunter Narr, 1988), pp. 355–94.

[3]There are five exceptions. *Break, great, steak, yea,* and *drain,* with ME [ɛ:] are still pronounced [e:], like ME [ɑ:] words.

which the variant [e:] for these words already existed in Middle English.[4] Another hypothesis, by William Labov and Geoffrey Nunberg, is that ME [ɛ:] and [ɑ:] merged *perceptually,* so that they were heard as homophones. The two sounds remained distinct *phonetically,* however, and when ME [ɛ:] eventually shifted from [e:] to [i:], ME [ɑ:] went no further than [e:].[5]

As for approximate dates, change 1, the dipthongization of ME [i:] and [u:], occurred in the early fifteenth century and change 2, the raising of ME [e:] and [o:] to [i:] and [u:], by 1500. Change 3, the fronting of ME [ɑ:] to [æ:], in words like *name,* began before 1500 and was retained in careful speech until about 1650, after which [æ:] was generally raised to [ɛ:] (change 5), although earlier and later examples occur. The subsequent raising of the new vowel [ɛ:] to [e:], change 7, was rare before 1650 and did not become normal in Standard English until the early eighteenth century. Meanwhile, the original [ɛ:] from the Middle English, in words like *clean,* had already shifted to [e:], change 4, and (by the description presented here) remained phonetically distinct from the new [ɛ:] but close to it perceptually. The further raising to [i:], change 6, occurred at the end of the seventeeth century and had become general by the middle of the eighteenth. The lowering of the diphthong [əɪ] to present-day [ɑɪ] occurred perhaps by 1600 in the north but was not adopted in southern English until the eighteenth century. As for the back vowels, ME [o:], as in *root,* had become [u:] by 1500, and ME [ɔ:], as in *bone,* though shifting to [o:] in more advanced speech during the sixteenth century, still perhaps retained its Middle English value in more conservative speech until the third quarter of the seventeenth century.

8.5 NOUNS (§180)

1. From your knowledge of Old English and the processes of language change, explain why *horse* has the plurals it has in the following examples. The first is from the Anglo-Saxon period; the other two are from the Renaissance.

a. Ðā menn ðe swyftoste *hors* habbað
   the men   who swiftest   horses have

   Note: See the paradigm for *scēap* in §3.6.

_____

_____

b. Those thousand *horse* shall sweat with martial spoile (Marlowe, *1 Tamburlaine* 1.2.191)

   Note: See §3.5 (Genitive). Old English had the genitive plural *(hors-a)* in this structure, the genitive of measure. What happened to the *-a* in Middle English?

_____

_____

---

[4]Dobson, *op. cit.* II, 606–32, follows Henry C. Wyld in arguing that the shift to [i:] as a *sound change* occurred in a dialect other than Standard English, which then influenced the pronunciation of specific words in Standard English; if this is the case, which is by no means certain, then two dialects are conflated in the present description.

[5]"Appendix A: Two Problematic Mergers in the History of English," in W. Labov *et al.,* eds., *A Quantitative Study of Sound Change in Progress* (Philadelphia: U.S. Regional Survey, 1972), I, 276–97.

c. Spurre your proud *Horses* hard, and ride in blood (*Richard III* 5.3.340)

    Note: Consider the operation of analogy. Where would *-es* come from?

_____

_____

2. What is the source of *eine,* the plural of *eye,* in Shakespeare's third line below? Refer if necessary to §3.6, especially footnote 7. What is the source of the plural *eyes* in the second line? Why do you think that the archaic plural was used in the third line?

> Alas, he naught esteem's that face of thine,
> To which Loues eyes paies tributarie gazes,
> Nor thy soft handes, sweet lips, and crystal eine,
> Whose full perfection all the world amazes
>
>   (*Venus and Adonis* 631–34)

_____

_____

3. Say aloud and transcribe phonetically Shakespeare's pronunciation of the italicized words (which was probably the same as the present-day American pronunciation):

>   the bound and high curuet
> of *Marses* fierie steed
>
>   (*All's Well* 2.3.299–300)

_____

>   In Characters, as red as *Mars his* heart
> Inflam'd with Venus
>
>   (*Troilus* 5.2.164–65)

_____

4. How does the pronunciation of phrases such as those in question 3 help to explain the rise of the *his*-genitive?

_____

5. The italicized phrases below illustrate the way of forming the "group genitive" that became standard during the Renaissance. Convert the phrases into the patterns they likely would have taken two centuries earlier.

    Note: Instead of "The Wife of Bath's Tale," Chaucer said "The Wyves Tale of Bathe."

In breefe, we are *the king of Englands subjects*   (*King John* 2.1.267)
               England's

_____

That it may reach *the King of Perseas crowne*   (Marlowe, *1 Tamburlaine* 2.3.53)
             Persia's

_____

O, in *the Duke of Glousters purse*   (*Richard III* 1.4.131)
          Gloucester's

_____

8.6 ADJECTIVES (§181)

In present-day English the forms for the comparative and superlative degrees of adjectives generally depend on the number of syllables in the uninflected form and on the weight of the second syllable in words of two syllables. Monosyllabic adjectives usually take the endings -er and -est, and most words of more than one syllable form the comparative and superlative with more and most (although two-syllable words with a light second syllable can take -er and -est: happy, happier; and monosyllabic words still occur with more and most.) Note the deviations from current usage in each of the adjectives in the following lines from Spenser, Marlowe, and Shakespeare.

1. So, now it is *more surer* on my head.   (Marlowe, *1 Tamburlaine* 2.7.65)
2. And I haue learn'd by the *perfect'st* report   (*Macbeth* 1.5.2)
3. Ingratitude, *more strong* then Traitors armes   (*Julius Caesar* 3.2.189)
4. Much greater griefe and *shamefuller* regrett   (Spenser, *Faerie Queene* 4.11.15.4)
5. Their lims *more large* and of a bigger size   (Marlowe, *1 Tamburlaine* 3.3.108)
6.   Dispose of her
    To some *more fitter* place; and that with speed   (*Measure for Measure* 2.2.17)
7. Silence is the *perfectest* Herault of ioy   (*Much Ado* 2.1.317)
8. To take the basest, and *most poorest* shape   (*Lear* 2.3.7)
9.   This is *more strange*
    Then such a murther is   (*Macbeth* 3.4.82)
10. Harbour more craft, and *more corrupter* ends   (*Lear* 2.2.108)
11. He, and Auffidius can no more attone
    Then *violent'st* Contrariety   (*Coriolanus* 4.6.73)
12. Therefore to make his entraunce *more sweet*,
    Heere, say wee drinke this standing boule of wine to him   (*Pericles* 2.3.64–65)

For each example above, write its number and its adjective in the blank following the phrase that describes the type of deviation from current usage.

Double comparative or superlative: _____

_____

_____

Inflectional -er or -est with word of more than one syllable: _____

_____

_____

More or *most* with monosyllable: _____

_____

_____

8.7 PRONOUNS (§182)

The continued use of the historical singular and plural forms for the second person pronoun allowed Renaissance English certain stylistic possibilities that present-day English has lost. The *th-* forms of the singular *(thou, thee, thy, thine)* were regularly used by persons of higher rank addressing an inferior, by parents speaking to a child, and by lovers or spouses in situations of intimacy. The singular form was also used by strangers regardless of rank to express anger or contempt. The *y-* forms *(you, ye, your, yours)* were used by persons of lower rank to a superior and by children to a parent. The emotionally more neutral *y-* forms could appropriately replace the *th-* forms in many situations, although the reverse was not true. As with French *tu* and *vous,* the plural form was the safer one in situations of uncertainty. Even the plural, however, could be emotionally charged when a person of higher rank addressed an inferior contemptuously, especially with an ironic *sir.* Explain briefly why the choice of pronoun is singular or plural in the following examples from Shakespeare.

[The first meeting between Romeo and Juliet, at the ball.]

JULIET. Good Pilgrime, *you* do wrong *your* hand too much,
Which mannerly deuotion shewes in this, 100
For Saints haue hands, that Pilgrims hands do tuch,
And palme to palme, is holy Palmers kisse.
ROMEO. Haue not Saints lips, and holy Palmers too?
JULIET. I pilgrim, lips that they must vse in prayer.
ROMEO. O then deare Saint, let lips do what hands do,
They pray (grant *thou*) lest faith turne to dispaire.
JULIET. Saints do not moue, though grant for prayers sake.
ROMEO. Then moue not while my prayers effect I take:
Thus from my lips, by *thine* my sin is purg'd.
JULIET. Then haue my lips the sin that they haue tooke. 110
ROMEO. Sin from my lips? O trespasse sweetly vrg'd:
Giue me my sin againe.
JULIET. *You* kisse by'th'booke.

(*Romeo and Juliet* 1.5.99–112)

_____

_____

_____

[The second meeting between Romeo and Juliet, at her balcony.]

JULIET. O Romeo, Romeo, wherefore art *thou* Romeo?
Denie *thy* Father and refuse *thy* name:
Or if *thou* wilt not, be but sworne my Loue,
And Ile no longer be a Capulet.
ROMEO. Shall I heare more, or shall I speake at this?

JULIET.   'Tis but *thy* name that is my Enemy:
             Thou are thy selfe, though not a Mountague....
                      Romeo, doffe *thy* name
             And for *thy* name which is no part of *thee,*
             Take all my selfe.
ROMEO.   I take *thee* at *thy* word:
             Call me but Loue, and Ile be new baptiz'd,   50
             Hence foorth I neuer will be Romeo.
JULIET.   What man art *thou,* that thus bescreen'd in night
             So stumblest on my counsell?
ROMEO.   By a name,
             I know not how to tell *thee* who I am:
             My name deare Saint, is hatefull to my selfe,
             Because it is an Enemy to *thee,*
             Had I it written, I would teare the word.
JULIET.   My ears haue yet not drunke a hundred words
             Of *thy* tongues vttering, yet I know the sound.
             Art *thou* not Romeo, and a Montague?   60

                      (*Romeo and Juliet* 2.2.33–39, 47–60)

[Talbot and his son John before a battle.]

TALBOT.   Vpon my Blessing I command *thee* goe.
JOHN.   To fight I will, but not to flye the Foe.
TALBOT.   Part of *thy* Father may be sau'd in thee.
JOHN.   No part of him, but will be shame in mee.
TALBOT.   *Thou* neuer hadst Renowne, nor canst not lose it.   40
JOHN.   Yes, *your* renowned Name: shall flight abuse it?
TALBOT.   *Thy* Fathers charge shal cleare thee from y^t staine.
JOHN.   *You* cannot witnesse for me, being slaine.

                      (*1 Henry VI* 4.5.36–43)

[The Duke of Clarence in prison and two men sent to murder him.]

CLARENCE.   Where art *thou* Keeper? Giue me a cup of wine.
2ND MURD.   *You* shall haue Wine enough my Lord anon.
CLARENCE.   In Gods name, what art *thou?*
1ST MURD.   A man, as *you* are.   170
CLARENCE.   But not as I am Royall.
1ST MURD.   Nor *you* as we are, Loyall.

CLARENCE.	*Thy* voice is Thunder, but *thy* looks are humble....	
1ST MURD.	What we will do, we do vpon command.	
2ND MURD.	And he that hath commanded, is our King.	
CLARENCE.	Erroneous Vassals, the great King of Kings	200

CLARENCE. Erroneous Vassals, the great King of Kings   200
Hath in the Table of his Law commanded
That *thou* shalt do no murther. Will *you* then
Spurne at his Edict, and fulfill a Mans?
Take heed: for he holds Vengeance in his hand,
To hurle vpon their heads that breake his Law.

2ND MURD. And that same Vengeance doth he hurle on *thee,*
For false Forswearing, and for murther too:
Thou did'st receiue the Sacrament, to fight
In quarrell of the House of Lancaster.

1ST MURD. And like a Traitor to the name of God,   210
Did'st breake that Vow, and with *thy* treacherous blade,
Vnrip'st the Bowels of *thy* Sou'raignes Sonne.

2ND MURD. Whom *thou* was't sworne to cherish and defend.

1ST MURD. How canst *thou* vrge Gods dreadfull Law to vs,
When *thou* hast broke it in such deere degree?

(*Richard III* 1.4.167–73, 198–215)

[Two enemies on the battlefield, Prince Hal and Henry Percy, surnamed Hotspur.]

HOTSPUR. If I mistake not, *thou* art Harry Monmouth.

PRINCE. *Thou* speak'st as if I would deny my name.   60

HOTSPUR. My name is Harrie Percie.

PRINCE.   Why then I see
A very valiant rebel of that name.
I am the Prince of Wales, and thinke not Percy,
To share with me in glory any more:
Two Starres keepe not their motion in one Sphere,
Nor can one England brooke a double reigne,
Of Harry Percy, and the Prince of Wales.

HOTSPUR. Nor shall it Harry, for the houre is come
To end the one of vs; and would to heauen,
Thy name in Armes, were now as great as mine.   70

PRINCE. Ile make it greater, ere I part from *thee,*
And all the budding Honors on *thy* Crest,
Ile crop, to make a Garland for my head.

HOTSPUR. I can no longer brooke *thy* Vanities.   *Fight.*

(*1 Henry IV* 5.4.59–74)

[Othello and Desdemona, immediately before her death.]

DESDEMONA.	Who's there? Othello?
OTHELLO.	I Desdemona.
DESDEMONA.	Will *you* come to bed, my Lord?
OTHELLO.	Haue *you* pray'd to night, Desdemon?
DESDEMONA.	I my Lord.
OTHELLO.	If *you* bethinke *your* selfe of any Crime
	Vnreconcil'd as yet to Heauen, and Grace,
	Solicite for it straight.
DESDEMONA.	Alacke, my Lord, what may *you* meane by that?
OTHELLO.	Well, do it, and be breefe, I will walke by:
	I would not kill *thy* vnprepared Spirit,
	No, Heauens fore-fend! I would not kill *thy* Soule.
DESDEMONA.	Talke *you* of killing?
OTHELLO.	I, I do.
DESDEMONA.	Then Heauen
	Haue mercy on mee.
OTHELLO.	Amen, with all my heart.
DESDEMONA.	If *you* say, I hope *you* will not kill me.
OTHELLO.	Humh.
DESDEMONA.	And yet I feare *you:* for *you're* fatall then
	When *your* eyes rowle so. Why I should feare, I know not,
	Since guiltinesse I know not: But yet I feele I feare.
OTHELLO.	Thinke on *thy* sinnes.
DESDEMONA.	They are Loues I beare to *you.*
OTHELLO.	I, and for that *thou* dy'st.

30

40

(*Othello* 5.2.23–40)

_____

_____

_____

[Two tribunes, Flavius and Murellus, and "certaine Commoners ouer the Stage."]

FLAVIUS.	Hence: home *you* idle Creatures, get *you* home:
	Is this a Holiday? What, know *you* not
	(Being Mechanicall) *you* ought not walke
	Vpon a labouring day, without the signe
	Of *your* Profession? Speake, what Trade art *thou?*
CARPENTER.	Why Sir, a Carpenter.
MURELLUS.	Where is *thy* Leather Apron, and *thy* Rule?
	What dost *thou* with *thy* best Apparrell on?
	You sir, what Trade are *you?*

COBLER.	Truely Sir, in respect of a fine Workman, I am but	10
	as *you* would say, a Cobler.	
MURELLUS.	But what Trade art *thou?* Answer me directly.	

(*Julius Caesar* 1.1.1–12)

8.8. PREPOSITIONS (§184)

For the following lines from Shakespeare write the preposition that would now be used instead of the italicized preposition.[6]

_____ 1. He came *of* an errand to mee, from Parson Hugh   (*Merry Wives* 1.4.80)

_____ 2. Therefore prepare your selfe *to* death   (*Measure for Measure* 3.1.169)

_____ 3. And be not iealous *on* me, gentle Brutus   (*Julius Caesar* 1.2.71)

_____ 4.   How? The Duke in Counsell?
In this time of the night?   (*Othello* 1.2.93)

_____ 5. I haue no power *vpon* you; Hers you are   (*Antony and Cleopatra* 1.3.23)

_____ 6.   Wee'l deliuer you
Of your great danger   (*Coriolanus* 5.6.14–15)

_____ 7. What thinke you *on*'t?   (*Hamlet* 1.1.55)

_____ 8. Like to a Ship, that hauing scap'd a Tempest,
Is straight way calme, and boorded *with* a Pyrate   (*2 Henry VI* 4.9.32–33)

_____ 9. That he which hath to stomack *to* this fight,
Let him depart   (*Henry V* 4.3.35–36)

_____ 10. Meet me in the palace wood, a mile *without* the Towne   (*Midsummer* 1.2.104)

_____ 11. They are, my Lord, *without* the Pallace Gate   (*Macbeth* 3.1.47)

_____ 12. *Grumio:* ... wee came downe a fowle hill, my Master riding behinde my Mistris.
Curtis: Both *of* one horse?   (*Taming of the Shrew* 4.1.69–71)

[6]These examples and many others are cited in E. A. Abbott, *A Shakespearian Grammar* (1870; reprint New York: Dover, 1966), pp. 93–139.

8.9 STRONG AND WEAK VERBS (§183)

The Middle English tendency for strong verbs to become weak continued during the Renaissance. A number of verbs that had been strong in Old English and that are now weak fluctuated between the two forms. A few weak verbs developed strong forms, but most of these, like all new verbs entering the language, are now exclusively weak, with -ed endings pronounced [d], [t], or [ɪd].

1. The italicized verbs are all in the past tense. Identify the forms as strong (S) or weak (W).

_____ 1. Three times to day I *holpe* him to his horse (*2 Henry VI* 5.3.8)

_____ 2. The first was I that *help'd* thee to the Crowne (*Richard III* 5.3.167)

_____ 3. The frame and huge foundation of the Earth
Shak'd like a Coward (*1 Henry IV* 3.1.16–17)

_____ 4. Oh, then the Earth *shooke* to see the Heauens on fire (*1 Henry IV* 3.1.25)

_____ 5. When the Sun *shyned* on the wyndowes there upon
(Kyd, *Housholders Philosophie*, 1408)

_____ 6. I: the most peerelesse peece of Earth, I thinke,
That ere the Sunne *shone* bright on (*Winter's Tale* 5.1.94–95)

_____ 7. Beheld them when they lighted, how they *clung*
In their Embracement (*Henry VIII* 1.1.9–10)

_____ 8. He on the suddaine *cling'd* her so about (Marlowe, *Hero and Leander* 2.314)

_____ 9. As to a stomack serv'd, whose insides meete,
Meate comes, it came; and *swole* our sailes (Donne, *Storme* 20–21)

_____ 10. And Sidnus *swell'd* aboue the Bankes (*Cymbeline* 2.4.71)

_____ 11. Many devout persons came and *sticked* in the dowy Image pretious
stones (Gage, *West Ind.* [1648], in *OED*)

_____ 12. He *stucke* them vp before the fulsome Ewes (*Merchant of Venice* 1.3.87)

_____ 13. Outward necessities…*drived* many to seek to Christ
(Baxter, *Paraphrase N. T.,* John 4.46 in OED)

_____ 14. A troubled mind *draue* me to walke abroad (*Romeo and Juliet* 1.1.127)

_____ 15. to behold he *clomb* up to the bancke (Spenser, *Faerie Queene* 2.7.57.1)

_____ 16. Make warre with him that *climb'd* vnto their nest (*3 Henry VI* 2.2.31)

2. The verbs in the sentences above had the following principal parts in Old English. Examine the vowels and endings of the principal parts to determine whether the Old English verbs were strong or weak, and write S or W in the first column. Then, from the sentences above, determine whether the verbs in Renaissance English were strong, weak, or variable, and write S, W, or S/W in the second column. Finally, from your own knowledge of present-day English, write S, W, or S/W in the last column to indicate that the verbs are strong, weak, or variable in current usage.

Old English				
helpan	'help'	healp	hulpon	holpen
scacan	'shake'	scōc	scōcon	scacen
scīnan	'shine'	scān	scinon	scinen
clingan	'cling'	clang	clungon	clungen
swellan	'swell'	sweal	swullon	swollen
stician	'stick'	sticode		sticod
drīfan	'drive'	drāf	drifon	drifen
climban	'climb'	clamb	clumbon	clumben

	Old English	Renaissance English	Present-Day English
help	S	S/W	W
shake			
shine			
cling			
swell			
stick			
drive			
climb			

8.10 QUESTIONS, NEGATIVES, AND THE AUXILIARY *DO* (§183)

In forming questions, negatives, and affirmative declarative sentences, writers of the Elizabethan period had more options available to them in the use of auxiliaries than did writers of either Middle English or later Modern English. The auxiliary *do* now occurs in nearly all negatives and yes-no questions that do not have another auxiliary verb or the verb *to be*. Before 1400 this use of *do* rarely occurred. The English of Shakespeare's period illustrates the transition of the usage at something like its mid-point. In 1600 as many as 80 percent of negative questions were formed by the newer pattern with *do* and only 20 percent by the older pattern without *do*.[7] Varying proportions occurred in other sentence types. Among affirmative questions approximately 60 percent contained *do* while 40 percent still used inversion alone. Among negative declarative sentences without other auxiliaries, 30 percent contained *do,* and 70 percent used the older pattern. A fourth construction, negative imperatives, contained *do* only about 20 percent of the time, the other 80 percent being of the *Forbid them not* type. And finally—a pattern that diverges from present usage in the opposite way—affirmative declara-

[7]The percentages for the various structures are from Alvar Ellegård, *The Auxiliary Do: The Establishment of Its Use in English* (Stockholm: Almqvist & Wiskell, 1953), p. 162. The quotations from Shakespeare are conveniently grouped (with many other examples) in F. T. Visser, *An Historical Syntax of the English Language* (Leiden: Brill, 1969), vol. III, pt. 1, pp. 1488–1571.

tive sentences that were not emphatic contained *do* about 5 percent of the time. This pattern never accounted for more than 10 percent of affirmative declarative sentences, and it died out at the beginning of the eighteenth century.

1. Write the number for each example below in the appropriate blanks to show how the various patterns are illustrated in Shakespeare.

	With *do*	Without *do*
Negative questions		
Affirmative questions		
Negative declaratives		
Negative imperatives		
Affirmative declaratives		

1. I do not sue to stand   (*Richard II* 5.3.129)
2. Or if there were, it not belongs to you   (*2 Henry IV* 4.1.98)
3. And did you leaue him in this contemplation?   (*As You Like It* 2.1.64)
4. O, doe not wish one more   (*Henry V* 4.3.33)
5. Andronicus, staine not thy Tombe with blood   (*Titus Andronicus* 1.1.116)
6. Who has the Office?   (*King Lear* 5.3.248)
7. Came he not home to night?   (*Romeo and Juliet* 2.4.2)
8. The Serpent that did sting thy Fathers life,
     Now weares his Crowne   (*Hamlet* 1.5.39–40)
9. Doe not ou loue me?   (*Much Ado* 5.4.74)
10. The King comes here to Night   (*Macbeth* 1.5.32)
11. What do you see?   (*Midsummer* 3.1.120)
12. What sayde he?   (*As You Like It* 3.2.221)
13. Sent he to Macduffe?   (*Macbeth* 3.6.39)

2. For each type of sentence that does not use *do,* describe the syntactic pattern by filling in the chart below. Give the number of the sentence illustrating each type and the order of the relevant parts from among Subject (S), Verb (V), Object (O), Negative (Neg), and Interrogative (Int). Indicate whether the pattern is still used.

Sentence Type without *do*	Number	Syntactic Pattern	Still Used?
Negative questions	7	Verb Subject Negative	No
Affirmative questions			
Affirmative questions			
Affirmative questions			
Negative declaratives			

Sentence Type without *do*	Number	Syntactic Pattern	Still Used?
Negative imperatives			
Affirmative declaratives			

3. You should have three sentences illustrating the affirmative question without *do*. One asks for a yes-no answer, the other two for additional information. The second type is often called a *WH question*. Write the number for each of the three sentences below, and indicate whether it is a yes-no or WH question.

_____

_____

4. There are two sentences illustrating the affirmative questions with *do*. Describe each of these syntactically by writing down the order of the relevant parts (Subject (S), Verb (V), Object (O), Interrogative (Int), Do/Did), and indicate whether it is a yes-no or WH

question. _____

_____

5. F. T. Visser[8] writes: "By and large the forms with *do* and those without *do* occurred side by side in the earlier centuries of the modern period, and the choice between the two possibilities seems to have been determined by rhythmical and stylistic considerations." With reference to affirmative questions, write a brief essay explaining the stylistic options that were available to an Elizabethan but are no longer available to a twentieth-century speaker of English.

8.11 THE LANGUAGE ILLUSTRATED[9]

King James Bible

The familiar *King James Bible,* or *Authorized Version,* of 1611 was the culmination of a series of translations during the preceding eighty years. Its style draws especially upon William Tyndale's translation into English of the Greek New Testament (1526) and the Hebrew Pentateuch (1530) and Miles Coverdale's translation of the remainder of the Old Testament, which he combined with Tyndale's work for a complete Bible in 1535. The *Authorized Version,* represented by the following two selections, was the happy result of a committee of 54 scholars appointed by King James in 1604.

[8]Ibid., p. 1545.

[9]See also the selections from Roger Ascham, Sir John Cheke, Richard Stanyhurst, Richard Mulcaster, John Chamberlain, James Howell, and Edward Phillips, in Baugh and Cable, Appendix B.

Moses and the Red Sea
Exodus 14.21–31

And Moses stretched out his hand ouer the Sea, and the Lord caused the Sea to goe backe by a strong East winde all that night, and made the Sea dry land, and the waters were diuided. And the children of Israel went into the midst of the Sea vpon the dry ground, and the waters were a wall vnto them on their right hand, and on their left. And the Egyptians pursued, and went in after them, to the midst of the Sea, euen all the Pharaohs horses, his charets and his horsemen. And it came to passe, that in the morning watch the Lord looked vnto the hoste of the Egyptians, through the pillar of fire, and of the cloude, and troubled the hoste of the Egyptians. And tooke off their charet wheeles, that they draue them heauily: So that the Egyptians said, Let vs flee from the face of Israel: for the Lord fighteth for them, against the Egyptians. And the Lord saide vnto Moses, Stretch out thine hand ouer the Sea, that the waters may come againe vpon the Egyptians, vpon their charets, and vpon their horsemen. And Moses stretched foorth his hand ouer the sea, and the sea returned to his strength when the morning appeared: and the Egyptians fled against it: and the Lord ouerthrew the Egyptians in the midst of the sea. And the waters returned, and couered the charets, and the horse-men, and all the hoste of Pharaoh that came into the sea after them: there remained not so much as one of them. But the children of Israel walked vpon drie land, in the midst of the sea, and the waters were a wall vnto them on their right hand, and on their left. Thus the Lord saued Israel that day out of the hand of the Egyptians: and Israel sawe the Egyptians dead vpon the sea shore. And Israel saw that great worke which the Lord did vpon the Egyptians: & the people feared the Lord, and beleeued the Lord, and his seruant Moses.

The Nativity
Luke 2.1–14

AND it came to passe in those dayes, that there went out a decree from Cesar Augustus, that all the world should be taxed. (And this taxing was first made whē Cyrenius was gouernor of Syria) And all went to bee taxed, euery one into his owne citie. And Joseph also wēt vp frō Galilee, out of the citie of Nazareth, into Judea, vnto the citie of Dauid, which is called Bethlehem, (because he was of the house and linage of Dauid,) To be taxed with Mary his espoused wife, being great with child. And so it was, that while they were there, the dayes were accomplished that she should be deliuered. And she brought foorth her first borne sonne, and wrapped him in swadling clothes, and laid him in a manger, because there was no roome for them in the Inne. And there were in the same countrey shepheards abiding in y̆ field, keeping watch ouer their flocke by night. And loe, the Angel of the Lord came vpon them, and the glory of the Lord shone round about them, and they were sore afraid. And the Angel said vnto them, Feare not: For behold, I bring you good tidings of great ioy, which shall be to all people. For vnto you is borne this day, in the citie of Dauid, a Sauiour, which is Christ the Lord. And this shall be a signe vnto you; yee shall find the babe wrapped in swadling clothes lying in a manger. And suddenly there was with the Angel a multitude of the heauenly hoste prais-ing God, and saying, Glory to God in the highest, and on earth peace, good wil towards men.

Shakespeare

Because Shakespeare's stylistic development was a continuing one, each play offers evidence not only of Renaissance English but also of the playwright's changing experiments with the language. *Macbeth* (c. 1606–1607) shows Shakespeare's style at a mature midpoint; measured by the technicalities of verse craft, it contrasts with the plays a decade and a half earlier as well as with those at the end of his career. *Macbeth* as a whole, for example, has nearly three times as high a proportion of run-on lines as the earlier *Richard III* (c. 1591–1594), though not yet as many as *The Tempest* (c. 1610–1611). Similarly, *Macbeth* has less rhyme than *Richard III,* though more than *The Tempest,* which has almost none at all. In *Macbeth,* more lines end on weakly stressed words (conjunctions, prepositions, auxiliary verbs, etc.) than in the earlier plays; and again Shakespeare's continuing stylistic experimentation is traceable, for his last seven plays all exceed *Macbeth* in this late characteristic of his art.[10]

Macbeth 1.7.1–82

MACBETH.   If it were done, when 'tis done, then 'twer well,
It were done quickly: If th'Assassination
Could trammell vp the Consequence, and catch
With his surcease, Successe: that but this blow
Might be the be all, and the end all. Heere,
But heere, vpon this Banke and Schoole of time,
Wee'ld iumpe the life to come. But in these Cases,
We still haue iudgement heere, that we but teach
Bloody Instructions, which being taught, returne
To plague th'Inuenter. This euen-handed Iustice   10
Commends th'Ingredience of our poyson'd Challice
To our owne lips. Hee's heere in double trust;
First, as I am his Kinsman, and his Subiect,
Strong both against the Deed: Then, as his Host,
Who should against his Murtherer shut the doore,
Not beare the knife my selfe. Besides, this *Duncane*
Hath borne his Faculties so meeke; hath bin
So cleere in his great Office, that his Vertues
Will pleade like Angels, Trumpet-tongu'd against
The deepe damnation of his taking off: 20
And Pitty, like a naked New-borne-Babe,
Striding the blast, or Heauens Cherubin, hors'd
Vpon the sightlesse Curriors of the Ayre,
Shall blow the horrid deed in euery eye,
That teares shall drowne the winde. I haue no Spurre
To pricke the sides of my intent, but onely
Vaulting Ambition, which ore-leapes it selfe
And falles on th'other.

Enter Lady.

                     How now? What Newes?
LADY MACBETH.   He has almost supt: why haue you left the chamber?
MACBETH.   Hath he ask'd for me?
LADY MACBETH.   Know you not, he ha's?   30
MACBETH.   We will proceed no further in this Businesse:
He hath Honour'd me of late, and I haue bought
Golden Opinions from all sorts of people,

---

[10]For these and other stylistic features of Shakespeare's plays, see David Bevington, ed., *The Complete Works of Shakespeare,* 3rd ed. (Glenview, Ill: Scott, Foresman, 1980), p. 72.

Which would be worne now in their newest glosse,
Not cast aside so soone.

LADY MACBETH.   Was the hope drunke,
Wherein you drest your selfe? Hath it slept since?
And wakes it now to looke so greene, and pale,
At what it did so freely? From this time,
Such I account thy loue. Art thou affear'd
To be the same in thine owne Act, and Valour,   40
As thou art in desire? Would'st thou haue that
Which thou esteem'st the Ornament of Life,
And liue a Coward in thine own Esteeme?
Letting I dare not, wait vpon I would,
Like the poore Cat i'th'Addage.

MACBETH.   Prythee peace:
I dare do all that may become a man,
Who dares no more, is none.

LADY MACBETH.   What Beast was't then
That made you breake this enterprize to me?
When you durst do it, then you were a man:
And to be more then what you were, you would   50
Be so much more the man. Nor time, nor place
Did then adhere, and yet you would make both:
They haue made themselues, and that their fitnesse now
Do's vnmake you. I haue giuen Sucke, and know
How tender 'tis to loue the Babe that milkes me,
I would, while it was smyling in my Face,
Haue pluckt my Nipple from his Bonelesse Gummes,
And dasht the Braines out, had I so sworne
As you haue done to this.

MACBETH.   If we should faile?
LADY MACBETH.   We faile?
But screw your courage to the sticking place,   60
And wee'le not fayle: when *Duncan* is asleepe,
(Whereto the rather shall his dayes hard Iourney
Soundly inuite him) his two Chanberlaines
Will I with Wine, and Wassell, so conuince,
That Memorie, the Warder of the Braine,
Shall be a Fume, and the Receit of Reason
A Lymbeck onely: when in Swinish sleepe,
Their drenched Natures lyes as in a Death,
What cannot you and I performe vpon
Th'vnguarded *Duncan?* What not put vpon   70
His spungie Officers? who shall bear the guilt
Of our great quell.

MACBETH.   Bring forth Men-Children onely:
For thy vndaunted Mettle should compose
Nothing but Males. Will it not be receiu'd,
When we haue mark'd with blood those sleepie two
Of his owne Chamber, and vs'd their very Daggers,
That they haue don't?

LADY MACBETH.   Who dares receiue it other,
As we shall make our Griefes and Clamor rore,
Vpon his Death?
MACBETH.   I am settled, and bend vp
Each corporall Agent to this terrible Feat.   80
Away, and mock the time with fairest show,
False Face must hide what the False Heart doth know.

Exeunt.

9

The Appeal to Authority, 1650–1800

9.1 QUESTIONS FOR REVIEW

1. Explain why the following people are important in historical discussions of the English language:

John Dryden
Jonathan Swift
Samual Johnson
Joseph Priestley
Robert Lowth
Lindley Murray
John Wilkins
James Harris
Thomas Sheridan
George Campbell

2. How were the intellectual tendencies of the eighteenth century reflected in attitudes toward the English language?

3. What did eighteenth-century writers mean by *ascertainment* of the English language? What means did they have in mind?

4. What kinds of "corruptions" in the English language did Swift object to? Do you find them objectionable? Can you think of similar objections made by commentators today?

5. What had been accomplished in Italy and France during the seventeenth century to serve as an inspiration for those in England who were concerned with the English language?

6. Who were among the supporters of an English Academy? When did the movement reach its culmination?

7. Why did an English Academy fail to materialize? What served as substitutes for an academy in England?

8. What did Johnson hope for his *Dictionary* to accomplish?

9. What were the aims of the eighteenth-century prescriptive grammarians?

10. How would you characterize the difference in attitude between Robert Lowth's *Short Introduction to English Grammar* (1762) and Joseph Priestley's *Rudiments of English Grammar* (1761)? Which was more influential?

11. How did prescriptive grammarians such as Lowth arrive at their rules?

12. What were some of the weaknesses of the early grammarians?

13. Which foreign language contributed the most words to English during the eighteenth century?

14. In tracing the growth of progressive verb forms since the eighteenth century, what earlier patterns are especially important?

15. Give an example of the progressive passive. From what period can we date its development?

9.2 JOHNSON'S DICTIONARY (§197)

Samuel Johnson's *Dictionary of the English Language* (1755) gave his age the standard and standardizing dictionary that it demanded.[1] On matters of usage that were controversial or on which Johnson himself had strong opinions, he did not hesitate to make pronouncements. These notes on usage, some original with Johnson, are important for reflecting the concerns of his age and for demonstrating how they differed both from the practice of writers of the preceding century and from the goals of lexicographers of the next.

In Baugh and Cable §185, we saw that Shakespeare often shifted words from one part of speech to another—nouns to verbs, verbs to nouns, adjectives to adverbs, and so on. Although this disposition to attempt the untried is characteristic of Shakespeare's time, it is not generally approved in Johnson's, and accordingly Johnson is bluntly critical of the free handling of the customary parts of speech. In illustrating the disapproved usages with citations from Shakespeare and Milton, Johnson makes clear that he follows his own preferences when they conflict with the practice of reputable writers, and in this, too, he is typical of his age. Under the letter *p*, for example, Johnson makes ten specific criticisms concerning shifts in parts of speech, in the entries below.[2]

Verb from Noun

To Period.   *v. a.*[3] [from the noun.] To put an end to. A bad word. [Quotation from Shakespeare]

To Pleasure.   *v. a.* [from the noun.] To please; to gratify. This word, though supported by good authority, is, I think, inelegant. [Quotations from Thomas Tusser, Shakespeare (twice), Francis Bacon, John Tillotson]

To Powder.   *v. n.* To come tumultuously and violently. A low corrupt word. [Quotation from Roger L'Estrange]

To Procession.   *v. n.* [from the noun.] To go in procession. A low word.

---

[1]See James H. Sledd and Gwin J. Kolb, *Dr. Johnson's Dictionary: Essays in the Biography of a Book* (Chicago: University of Chicago Press, 1955), pp. 1–45.

[2]From Harold B. Allen, "Samuel Johnson and the Authoritarian Principle in Linguistic Criticism," Diss. University of Michigan 1940, pp. 294–300.

[3]Johnson's abbreviations *v. a.* stand for *verb active* (transitive), *v. n.* for *verb neuter* (intransitive), and *n. s.* for *noun substantive*.

To Profound. *v. n.* [from the noun.] To dive; to penetrate. A barbarous word. [Quotation from Joseph Glanvill]

To Proselyte. *v. a.* To convert. A bad word. [Quotation from *Government of the Tongue*]

To Proverb. *v. a.* [from the noun.] Not a good word. [Quotations from Milton and Shakespeare]

Adjective from Noun

Plenty. *n. s.* . . . 3. It is used, I think, barbarously for *plentiful.* [Quotations from Thomas Tusser and Shakespeare]

Noun from Adverb

Peradventure. adv. . . . 2. Doubt; question. It is sometimes used as a noun, but not gracefully or properly. [Quotation from Robert South]

Noun from Verb

Proceed. *n. s.* [from the verb.] Produce: as, *the* proceeds *of an estate. Clarissa.* Not an imitable word, though much used in law writings.

Check each word in the *Oxford English Dictionary* under its derived part of speech (the first seven under *verb*, **plenty** under *adjective,* and **peradventure** and **proceed** under *noun* or *substantive*). If there are several meanings, check the meaning that is closest to the one that Johnson gives. Write the usage label from the *OED,* if any *(colloquial, dialectal, obsolete, rare),* and the date of the latest illustrative quotation. Then check your own collegiate dictionary to determine whether the word is listed under the same part of speech and meaning that Johnson gives and its usage label, if any.

To what extent are Johnson's preferences shared by later dictionaries? _____

	OED Usage Label	*OED* Date of Latest Quotation	Usage Label in Your Dictionary
period, *v.*			
pleasure, *v.*			
powder, *v.*			
procession, *v.*			

	OED Usage Label	*OED* Date of Latest Quotation	Usage Label in Your Dictionary
profound, *v.*			
proselyte, *v.*			
proverb, *v.*			
plenty, *adj.*			
peradventure, *sb.*			
proceed, *sb.*			

9.3 UNIVERSAL GRAMMAR (§198)

James Harris's *Hermes: or, a Philosophical Inquiry concerning Language and Universal Grammar* (1751) is an impressively logical statement of the goals and methods of linguistic inquiry and a penetrating attempt to attain those goals. Unlike most grammarians of his century, Harris was concerned with the study of language in its own right as a science, not as a means of purifying the language—and he was followed in this concern during the next thirty years by distinguished writers on the subject such as Joseph Priestley, Adam Smith, and Lord Monboddo. In the present century transformational grammarians have seen Harris's philosophically oriented work as a precursor of their own investigations.[4]

The first two of the following excerpts, from Book I, Chapter I and Book I, Chapter II, define universal grammar and explain its goals. The excerpts on pronouns, articles, and prepositions illustrate Harris's method of discovering the logical structure of language by relating it to the structure of the world. The final passage, from Book III, Chapter IV, is a discussion of language and mind.

From Book I, Chapter I
Introduction. Design of the Whole

IF Men by nature had been framed for Solitude, they had never felt an Impulse to converse one with another. And if, like lower Animals, they had been by nature irrational, they could not have recogniz'd the proper Subjects of Discourse. Since SPEECH then is the joint Energie of our best and noblest Faculties . . . (that is to say, of our *Reason* and our *social Affection*) being withal our *peculiar* Ornament and Distinction, as *Men;* those Inquiries may surely be deemed interesting as well as

---

[4]For a good survey of eighteenth-century grammars that departed from the familiar prescriptive goals, see Scott Elledge, "The Naked Science of Language, 1747–1786," in *Studies in Criticism and Aesthetics, 1660–1880: Essays in Honor of Samuel Holt Monk,* ed. Howard Anderson and John S. Shea (Minneapolis: University of Minnesota Press, 1967), pp. 266–95.

liberal, which either show how SPEECH may be naturally *resolved;* or how, when resolved, it may be again *combined.*

HERE a large field for speculating opens before us. We may either behold SPEECH, as divided into *its constituent Parts,* as a Statue may be divided into its several Limbs; or else, as resolved into its *Matter* and *Form,* as the same Statue may be resolved into its Marble and Figure.

THESE different *Analyzings* or *Resolutions* constitute what we call PHILOSOPHICAL, or UNIVERSAL GRAMMAR.

When we have viewed SPEECH thus *analyzed,* we may then consider it, as *compounded.* And here is the first place we may contemplate . . . *Synthesis,* which *by combining simple Terms* produces a *Truth;* then by *combining two Truths* produces a *third;* and thus others, and others, in continued Demonstration, till we are led, as by a road, into the regions of SCIENCE.

From Book I, Chapter II
Concerning the Analysing of Speech into its smallest Parts

THUS in SPEECH for example—All men, even the lowest, can speak their Mother-Tongue. Yet how many of this multitude can neither write, nor even read? How many of those, who are thus far literate, knowing nothing of that Grammar, which respects the Genius of their own Language? How few then must be those, who know GRAMMAR UNIVERSAL; *that Grammar,* which without regarding the several Idioms of particular Languages, *only respects those Principles, that are essential to them all?* . . .

If then the *Soul's leading Powers* be *the two* above mention'd [perception and volition], and it be true that *all Speech is a publication of these Powers,* it will follow that EVERY SENTENCE WILL BE EITHER A SENTENCE OF ASSERTION, OR A SENTENCE OF VOLITION. And thus, by referring all of them to one of these two classes, have we found an expedient to reduce their infinitude.

From Book I, Chapter V
Concerning Substantives of the Secondary Order

BUT tho' all these Pronouns have *Number,* it does not appear either in *Greek,* or *Latin,* or any modern Language, that those of the first and second Person carry the distinctions of SEX. The reason seems to be, that the Speaker and Hearer being generally present to each other, it would have been superfluous to have mark'd a distinction by Art, which from Nature and even Dress was commonly . . . apparent on both sides. But this does not hold with respect to the third Person, of whose Character and Distinctions (including SEX among the rest) we often know no more, than what we learn from the discourse. And hence it is that in most Languages *the third Person* has its *Genders,* and that even *English* (which allows its Adjectives no Gender at all) has in this Pronoun the triple . . . distinction of *He, She,* and *It.*

HENCE too we see the reason why *a single Pronoun* . . . to each Person, an I to the *First,* and a *Thou* to the *Second,* are abundantly sufficient to all the purposes of Speech. But 'tis not so with respect to the *Third* Person. The various relations of the various Objects exhibited by this (I mean relations of near and distant, present and absent, same and different, definite and indefinite, &c.) made it necessary that here there should not be one, but *many* Pronouns, such as *He, This, That, Other, Any, Some,* &c. . . .

As to the *Coalescence* of these Pronouns, it is, as follows. The first or Second will either of them by themselves coalesce with the Third, but not with each other. For example, 'tis good sense, as well as good Grammar, to say in any Language—I AM HE—THOU ART HE—but we cannot say, I AM THOU—nor THOU ART I. The reason is, there is no absurdity for the *Speaker* to be the *Subject* also of the Discourse, as when we say, **I AM HE;** or for the *Person addrest;* as when we say, **THOU ART HE.** But for the same Person, in the same circumstances, to be at once the Speaker, and the Party addrest, this is impossible; and so therefore is the Coalescence of the First and Second Person. . . .

From Book II, Chapter I
Concerning Definitives

BUT this is not enough. The Thing, at which we are looking, is neither a Species, nor a Genus. What is it then? An Individual.—Of what kind? *Known,* or *unknown?* Seen now *for the first time,* or *seen before,* and now remembered?—'Tis here we shall discover the use of the two Articles (A) and (THE.) (A) respects our *primary* Perception, and denotes individuals as *unknown;* (THE) respects our *secondary* Perception, and denotes Individuals as *known.* To explain by an example—I see an object pass by, which I never saw till then. What do I say?—*There goes* A *Beggar, with* A *long Beard. The Man departs, and returns a week after. What do I say then?—There goes* THE *Beggar with* THE *long Beard.* The Article only is changed, the rest remains un-altered.

YET mark the force of this apparently minute Change. The Individual, *once vague,* is now recognized *as something known,* and that merely by the efficacy of this latter Article, which tacitly insinuates a kind of *previous* acquaintance, by referring the present Perception to a like Perception already past. . . .

THE ARTICLES already mentioned are those *strictly* so called; but besides these there are the PRONOMINAL ARTICLES such as *This, That, Any, Other, Some, All, No,* or *None,* &c. Of these we have spoken already in our Chapter of Pronouns . . . where we have shewn, when they may be taken as Pronouns, and when as Articles. Yet in truth it must be confessed, if the Essence of an Article be *to define* and *ascertain,* they are much more properly Articles, than any thing else, and as such should be considered in Universal Grammar. Thus when we say, THIS *Picture I approve, but* THAT *I dislike,* what do we perform by the help of these Definitives, but bring down the common Appellative, to denote two Individuals, the one as *the more near,* the other as *the more distant?*

From Book II, Chapter III
Concerning Those Connectives, Called Prepositions

SOME things co-alesce and unite *of themselves;* others refuse to do so *without help,* and as it were compulsion. Thus in Works of Art, the Mortar and the Stone co-alesce of themselves; but the Wainscot and the Wall not without Nails and Pins. In Nature this is more conspicuous. For example; all Quantities and Qualities co-alesce immediately with their Substances. Thus 'tis we say, *a fierce Lion, a vast Mountain;* and from this *Natural Concord of Subject and Accident,* arises *the Grammatical Concord of Substantive and Adjective.* . . .

THE general Conclusion appears to be this. "THOSE PARTS OF SPEECH UNITE OF THEMSELVES IN GRAMMAR, WHOSE ORIGINAL ARCHETYPES UNITE OF THEMSELVES IN NATURE."

. . . Here then we perceive the Rise and Use of PREPOSITIONS. By these we connect those Substantives to Sentences, which at the time are unable to co-alesce *of themselves.* Let us assume for instance a pair of these Connectives, THRO' and, WITH, and mark their Effect upon the Substances here mentioned. *The splendid Sun* WITH *his Beams genially warmeth* THRO' *the Air the fertile Earth.* The Sentence, as before, remains *intire and one;* the *Substantives* required, are both *introduced;* and not a Word, which was there before, is detruded from its proper place.

From Book III, Chapter IV
Concerning general or universal ideas

IN short ALL MINDS, that are, are SIMILAR and CONGENIAL; and so too are *their Ideas,* or *intelligible Forms.* Were it otherwise, there could be no intercourse between Man and Man, or (what is more important) between Man and God.

FOR what is Conservation between Man and Man?—'Tis a mutual intercourse of *Speaking* and *Hearing.*—To the Speaker, 'tis *to teach;* to the Hearer, 'tis *to learn.*—To the Speaker, 'tis *to descend* from *Ideas* to *Words;* to the Hearer, 'tis *to ascend* from *Words* to *Ideas.*—If the Hearer, in this ascent, can arrive at *no* Ideas, then is he said *not to understand;* if he ascend to Ideas dissimilar and heterogeneous, then is he said *to misunderstand.—* What then is requisite, that he may be said *to understand?*—That he should ascend to certain Ideas, treasured up *within himself,* correspondent and similar to those *within the Speaker.* The same may be said of a *Writer* and a *Reader;* as when any one reads to day or to morrow, or here or in *Italy,* what *Euclid* wrote in *Greece* two thousand years ago.

Now is it not marvelous, there should be *so exact an Identity of our Ideas,* if they were only generated from *sensible* Objects, infinite in number, ever changing, distant in Time, distant in Place, and no one Particular with any other?

HAD we not better reason thus upon so abstruse a Subject?—Either all MINDS have their Ideas *derived;* or all have them *original;* or *some have them original, and some derived.* If all Minds have them derived, they must be derived from something, *which is itself not Mind,* and thus we fall insensibly into a kind of Atheism. If all have them original, *then are all Minds divine,* an Hypothesis by far more plausible than the former. But if this be not admitted, then must *one* Mind (at least) have *original* Ideas, and the rest have them *derived.* Now supposing this last, whence are those Minds, whose Ideas are derived, most likely to derive them?—From MIND, or from BODY?—From MIND, a thing *homogeneous;* or from BODY, a thing *heterogeneous?* From MIND, such as (from the Hypothesis) has *original ideas;* or from BODY, which we cannot discover to have any Ideas at all?—An Examination of this kind, pursued with accuracy and temper, is the most probable method of solving these doubts.

10

The Nineteenth Century and After

10.1 QUESTIONS FOR REVIEW

1. Explain why the following people are important in historical discussions of the English Language:

Sir James A. H. Murray
Henry Bradley
Sir William A. Craigie
C. T. Onions

2. Define the following terms and for each provide examples of words or meanings that have entered the English language since 1800:

Borrowing
Self-explaining compound
Compound formed from Greek or Latin elements
Prefix
Suffix
Coinage
Common word from proper name
Old word with new meaning
Extension of meaning
Narrowing of meaning
Degeneration of meaning
Regeneration of meaning
Slang
Verb-adverb combination

3. What distinction has been drawn between cultural levels and functional varieties of English? Do you find the distinction valid?

4. What are the principal regional dialects of English in the British Isles? What are some of the characteristics of these dialects?

5. What are the main national and areal varieties of English that have developed in countries that were once part of the British Empire?

6. Summarize the main efforts at spelling reform in England and the United States during the past century. Do you think that a movement for spelling reform will succeed in the future?

7. How long did it take to produce the *Oxford English Dictionary?* By what name was it originally known?

8. What changes have occurred in English grammatical forms and conventions during the past two centuries?

10.2 SELF-EXPLAINING COMPOUNDS (§217)

Although the process of forming self-explaining compounds is one of the oldest and most familiar methods of word formation in the language, a complete and consistent description of this process continues to challenge linguists. A *cleaning woman,* for example, is a woman who cleans. A *punching bag,* however, is not a bag that punches but a bag that is punched. And a *tuning fork* is neither a fork that tunes nor a fork that is tuned but an implement that is useful for tuning musical instruments. Finally, *swimming pool* has the form of none of these, for it indicates a place where swimming is done.

One study of compounds in English argues that most compounds can be derived from structures that contain one of the following nine words: *cause, have, make, use, be, in, for, from, about.*[1] Thus, *tear gas* can be derived from "gas which *causes* tears," and *horse doctor* from "doctor *for* a horse," with the understood words deleted.

1. Assign the compounds below to their appropriate categories by writing out for each the clause or phrase from which it can be derived.

disease germ   ghost story   hound dog
wood alcohol   city park   night flight
songbird   girl friend   nose drops
raisin bread   sleeping pill   apple butter
doghouse   gunboat   windmill
silkworm   air brake   sex scandal

Key Words	Compound	Underlying Structure
cause	(as in *tear gas*	gas which causes tears)
	_____	_____
	_____	_____
have	(as in *picture book*	book which has pictures)
	_____	_____
	_____	_____
make	(as in *honeybee*	bee which makes honey)
	_____	_____
	_____	_____

[1]Judith N. Levi, *The Syntax and Semantics of Complex Nominals* (New York: Academic Press, 1978).

Key Words	Compound	Underlying Structure
uses	(as *steamboat*	boat which uses steam)
be	(as in *pine tree*	tree which is a pine)
in	(as in *field mouse*	mouse in the field)
for	(as in *horse doctor*	doctor for a horse)
from	(as in *olive oil*	oil from olives)
about	(as in *tax law*	law about taxes)

10.3 COINAGES (§220)

1. Identify the words from which the following blends were formed, and underline the part of each word that was retained in the blend.

motel _____ + _____

smog _____ + _____

gasohol _____ + _____

sitcom _____ + _____

decathlete _____ + _____

fantabulous _____ + _____

Chunnel _____ + _____

Eurailpass _____ + _____

telethon _____ + _____

workaholic _____ + _____

slumlord _____ + _____

transceiver	_____	+	_____
Republicrat	_____	+	_____
sci-fi	_____	+	_____
simulcast	_____	+	_____
quasar	_____	+	_____
xeriscape	_____	+	_____

10.4 SLANG (§225)

In each set of slang terms and phrases below, circle the one item that doesn't belong. It will go with the next set. In your own words give the meaning of each set.[2]

1. catch with a smoking gun, have dead to rights, nail, rack out, catch redhanded

_____

2. catch Zs, connect the dots, bag it, hit the great white biscuit, flake out

_____

3. spell out, clue in, decode, bring someone up to speed, cope

_____

4. get by, talk turkey, muddle through, manage, squeak through

_____

5. bollix up, lay it on the line, get down to brass tacks, let it all hang out, pull no punches

_____

6. screw up, blow it, goof up, make a muck of, louse up, buzz off

_____

7. vamoose, put the skids on, haul ass, make like a paper doll and cut out, fly the coop

_____

8. take someone down a notch, cut off at the knees, take the wind out of someone's sails, Adonis

_____

9. hunk, beefcake, cabbage, collar ad, dreamboat

_____

10. bread, pig sweat, green stuff, lucre, moolah

_____

11. go-getter, white lightning, coffin varnish, rotgut, shoe polish

_____

[2]See Robert L. Chapman, *Thesaurus of American Slang* (New York: Harper & Row, 1989).

12. hot shot, eager beaver, yapper, live wire, cage rattler

_____

13. blabbermouth, gum-beater, windbag, yenta, shyster

_____

14. flimflammer, hustler, cold fish, con man, chiseler

_____

10.5 ENGLISH AS A WORLD LANGUAGE (§229)

The sentences below are taken from books written in Australia, India, West Africa, East Africa, South Africa, and the West Indies. Try to deduce the meanings of the words written below each sentence from the context, and then check the second edition or the online edition of the *Oxford English Dictionary.* If there is more than one entry, look under the part of speech used here. Write down the origin of the word (as printed in brackets, reached online by clicking Etymology) and its meaning. Words are italicized as in the original texts.

1. "Oy, mate, go inside and ask the Old Girl if you can put the billy on, will you?" [Colleen McCullough, *Tim* (New York: Harper and Row, 1974), p. 12.]

billy _____

_____

_____

2. "Want a bikkie, love?" she asked, extending the cookie jar. "I got some real grouse choccy ones in there." [*Ibid.,* p. 12.]

grouse _____

_____

_____

3. "Shut up, Curly, you drongo!" Ron snarled irritably. [*Ibid.,* p. 26.]

drongo _____

_____

_____

4. "Christ, why couldn't Dawnie have married a dinkum bloke instead of a simpering, stuck-up pansy like you?" [*Ibid.,* p. 145.]

dinkum _____

_____

_____

5. The larrikins avoided him. They loitered on the other side of the street. They had clashed with him and showed no desire to repeat the experience. [Ronald McKie, *The Mango Tree* (Sydney: Collins, 1974), p. 45.]

larrikin _____

_____

_____

6. They moved around in taxis and only stayed in the fancy ashrams. [Chaman Nahal, *Into Another Dawn* (New Delhi: Sterling Publishers Private, 1977), p. 47.]

ashram _____

_____

_____

7. "Are you asking this loafer, this goonda, to stay?" [*Ibid.,* p. 43.]

goonda _____

_____

_____

8. "This bloody atman business. The inner self and the outer self. Too confusing and complicated. No, not for me, brother, your religion!" [*Ibid.,* p. 49.]

atman _____

_____

_____

9. They ate palm nut soup, fufu, fried red plantain and nuts. [J. Benibengor Blay, *Coconut Boy* (n.p. Ghana: West African Publishing Co., 1970), p. 108.]

fufu _____

_____

_____

10. She adjusted her *lappa* so that the hem now rested on her bare feet. [I. N. C. Aniebo, *The Journey Within* (London, Heinemann, 1978), p. 23.]

lappa _____

_____

_____

11. The money they received from selling there was used to buy yams, bags of *garri* and other produce from the local farmers which was then taken back for sale in Lagos. [Buchi Emecheta, *The Bride Price* (London: Allison & Busby, 1976), p. 59.]

garri _____

_____

_____

12. "Why couldn't the *askaris* be stopped from arresting her brother?" [Bernard P. Chahilu, *The Herdsman's Daughter* (Nairobi: East African Publishing House, 1974), p. 81.]

askari _____

_____

_____

13. The market was still as it was when she last saw it. The *dukas* were the same dirty old buildings they used to be. . . . She went to one of the *dukas* to buy herself a bottle of Fanta. [*Ibid.,* p. 91.]

duka _____

_____

_____

14. Then suddenly, as if struck with an idea, he released the cattle from the *boma* and drove them away without saying a word to his wife in the house. [*Ibid.,* p. 5.]

boma _____

_____

_____

15. In the middle of the *manyatta,* which was a large *boma,* was a shed. [Edward Hinga, *Out of the Jungle* (Nairobi: East African Literature Bureau, 1973), p. 23.]

manyatta _____

_____

_____

16. The cattle were in the care of small Maasai boys. Two hundred well armed *morans* acted as guards. The tall *morans* walked fearlessly and I was reminded of their fearlessness in battle. [J. N. Mbugua, *Mumbi's Brideprice* (Nairobi: Longman, 1971), p. 37.]

moran _____

_____

_____

17. "Parse and analyse that sentence if you could, you old *macoumere.*" [Samuel Selvon, *The Housing Lark* (London: Macgibbon & Kee, 1965), p. 139.]

macoumere _____

_____

_____

_____

10.6 PIDGINS AND CREOLES (§230)

At the risk of giving the impression that pidgin and creole languages are simply more colorful and more concrete versions of a limited part of a standard language, this exercise focuses on metaphorical expressions in Cameroon Pidgin. It should be borne in mind that the metaphorical constructions of the lexicon are only part of the whole grammar of a pidgin or a creole language, and that other parts of the grammar, such as tense and aspect in the verbal system, make abstract distinctions that are not available in the standard language. Nevertheless, interesting patterns of the lexicon can be studied separately. As Loreto Todd writes, "[M]etaphor is an obvious means of extending the usefulness of a small vocabulary."[3]

Three sets of corresponding phrases, each in random order, are given below: **(1)** a simplified phonetic script for the phrase in the pidgin language, **(2)** the literal source in English, and **(3)** an English translation. Match the pidgin phrase with its English source and the English translation:

Cameroon Pidgin	Literal English Source	English Translation
trong hed		
drai ai		
mek yu lɔs faia		
han fɔ stik		
big hed		
swit mɔt		
biabia fɔ ai		
fut fɔ stik		
open han		
lɔk ai		
wuman han		
bele fulɔp		
wata fɔ stik		
blak hat		
motu fut		

[3]Loreto Todd, "Lexical Patterning in Cameroon Pidgin and Tok Pisin," in *Diversity and Development in English-related Creoles,* ed. Ian F. Hancock (Ann Arbor: Karoma, 1985), pp. 116–33.

Literal English Source	English Translation
big head	branch
motor foot	put the fire out
water for stick	flattery
black heart	eyebrow/lash
beard for eye	generous
make you lose fire	bottom of the tree
strong head	blindness
dry eye	pride
foot for stick	stubbornness
sweet mouth	car tire
open hand	really evil
hand for stick	satisfied stomach
lack eye	sap
belly full up	left hand
woman hand	unsympathetic, hard-hearted

10.7 GENDER ISSUES AND PRONOMINAL CHANGE (§233)

Even a grammatical system as stable as personal pronouns is subject to influence by social and cultural forces. See, for example, the distinctions in second person pronouns that changed first in one direction and then in another partly because of changing structures in social class (§§7.8 and 8.7). Recent observers of pronominal usage have noted that a desire for nonsexist language is bringing about a change in the paradigm toward the use of a plural pronoun with a singular antecedent instead of the masculine pronoun for both sexes, or from (A) to (B):

A.

Person	Number			
	Singular			Plural
1st	I			WE
2nd	YOU			
3rd	IT	SHE	HE	THEY

B.

Person	Number	
	Singular	Plural
1st	I	WE
2nd	YOU	
3rd	IT SHE HE	THEY

For example, compare "Anyone can do it if he tries hard enough" with "Anyone can do it if they try hard enough." Furthermore, these observers point out that paradigm B already reflects several centuries of usage in English literature, despite proscriptions of traditional grammarians to the contrary.[4] British usage has always accepted plural pronouns in these contexts more readily than American usage.

For each of the following sentences indicate whether the personal pronoun shows agreement in number but problematic reference to gender, as in (A); or lack of agreement in number and nonsexist usage in gender, as in (B).[5]

_____*B*_____ 1. How can *anybody* be happy while *they're* in perpetual fear of being seen and censured? (William Congreve, *Love for Love,* 1695)

_____ 2. But, you know, the more I love *anybody,* the more Lady O'Shane hates *them.* (Maria Edgeworth, *Ormond,* 1817)

_____ 3. What the laws of life demand of *everyone* is that *he* always do absolutely the best that *he* can under all circumstances. (John Dewey, *Essays,* 1903–06)

_____ 4. He was one of those precious men whom *everybody* would choose to work for *them.* (George Eliot, *Middlemarch,* 1874)

_____ 5. If *any person* demands better, *he* is at liberty to do so. (George Eliot, *Middlemarch,* 1874)

_____ 6. *Every person* has a right to take care of *themselves.* (Charles Dickens, *Christmas Carol,* 1843)

_____ 7. Clearly it is time
    To become disillusioned, *each person* to enter *his* own soul's desert
    And look for God,—having seen man.
                                (Robinson Jeffers, "The Soul's Desert," 1939)

[4]See Ann Bodine, "Androcentrism in Prescriptive Grammar: Singular 'they', sex-indefinite 'he', and 'he or she,'" *Language in Society,* 4 (1975), 129–46. Rpt. in *The Feminist Critique of Language: A Reader,* ed. Deborah Cameron, 2nd ed. (London: Routledge, 1998), pp. 124–38.

[5]For many additional examples, see H. Poutsma, *A Grammar of Late Modern English* (Groningen, Netherlands: Noordhoff, 1914), II, pt. 1A, 310–12; George H. McKnight, *Modern English in the Making* (New York: Appleton, 1928), pp. 528–30; and F. T. Visser, *An Historical Syntax of the English Language* (Leiden, Netherlands: Brill, 1963), I, 74–78.

_____ 8. A sound went through the court, produced by *each person* drawing in *their* breath hard, as men do when they expect or witness what is frightful, and the same time affecting. (Sir Walter Scott, *The Heart of Mid-Lothian,* 1818)

_____ 9. *Nobody* prevents you, do *they?* (W. M. Thackeray, *Pendennis,* 1848–50)

_____ 10. *Nobody* would be afraid if *he* could help it. (Tobias Smollett, *Sir Launcelot Greaves,* 1762)

_____ 11. *Nobody* meant to be unkind, but *nobody* put *themselves* out of their way to secure her comfort. (Jane Austen, *Mansfield Park,* 1814)

_____ 12. There is not *one* in a hundred of either sex who is not taken in when *they* marry. (Jane Austen, *Mansfield Park,* 1814)

10.8 THE LANGUAGE ILLUSTRATED (§§228–229)

Geordie

The Dialect of Newcastle-upon-Tyne known as Geordie is distinctive for its northern vocabulary and its Northumbrian burr. The burr is a pronunciation of *r* as a uvular fricative [ʁ], which contrasts both with the Scottish rolled *r* and the English frictionless *r* (the latter being lost before a consonant or in final position). The author of the following example describes the sound and instructs the reader in its pronunciation for four pages. He suggests at one point swabbing the tonsils with "an embrocation compounded of equal parts of surgical spirit and Madras Curry Powder (extra hot)" before attempting the Northumbrian *r*.[6]

Moses and the Red Sea

Noo the gaffer ov aal the Israelites was a chep caalled Moses and he fell oot wi' Pharaoh whe wez gaffer ov aal the Egyptians. So Moses sez to his lads, "Howway ower the Reed Sea." So they aall set oot wi' thor bairns and thor posstubs, whippets and galloways te plodge ower the watter. "Had on" sez Moses, "Had on". And he hoisted his deppity's stick up ahight. Whey man ye wadn't credit it. The watters parted. Thor wez a waall o' water on one side and a waall o' watter on the other. So thor wez ne caall to plodge ower. So off sets the Israelites ahint Moses and efter them, het-foot across the scaadin' het sands comes Pharaoh and his lads. "Hey up" sez Pharaoh "noo we've got them", and he gets his lads te whip up thor cuddies and they sets off te bray the Israelites—het foot across the scaadin' het sands—tappy lappy ower the bed o' the Reed Sea. Thor wez a waal o' watter on one side and a waal o' watter on t'other. They wor gannin' like the clappers—cuddies, brakes and sowljers—and man thor wor just aboot te bray the poor Israelites when Moses torns roond. He up wi' 'is deppity's stick hoyin' it reet up ahight. What a gan on—doon cum the waall o' watter on one side—doom cum the waall o' watter on t'other and ivery last bugger of the Egyptians wez drooned forbye the smallest one, young Ahmed, and he got his wellies stuck in the clarts.

Scots

Among the important features in which Modern Scots diverges from Modern English are the development of Old English *ā* into Scots [e] instead of [o] (as in Scots *hame,* Modern English

---

[6]Reprinted by permission of Frank Graham, from Scott Dobson, *Larn Yersel Geordie* (Newcastle-upon-Tyne: Frank Graham, 1969), p. 25.

home), the retention of [hw] in words like *wha* (Modern English *who*, Old English *hwā*), and the rolled *r*, which, unlike the English *r* is retained before a consonant. Wullie, the hero of the strip on the opposite page (see Figure 10.1), is from Aberdeen in northeastern Scotland.

Jamaican English

Recent scholarly attention to **pidgin** and **creole** languages has given linguists a better under-standing of the processes of language change and of the linguistic and sociological issues sur-rounding the varieties of English around the world. As the most thoroughly studied of the Caribbean varieties of the language, Jamaican English illustrates some of the linguistic prob-lems and certain key terms.

A **pidgin** is a language that has no native speakers; it serves as a means of limited com-munication when speakers of different languages come in contact—most typically, speakers of a West European language (Portuguese, Spanish, French, English) and a non-European lan-guage (Twi, Ibo, Hawaiian, etc.). Such a language is much reduced in structure and vocabulary compared with the languages from which it is derived; and most of its vocabulary comes from the language of the economically dominant group. The most fully pidginized systems appear to come about when several languages are in contact rather than just two. When the speakers of the next generation learn the pidgin as a native language and reexpand the structure and the vocabulary as necessary for their needs, the resulting language is a **creole.** Then if the language of subsequent generations moves in the direction of one of the languages upon which the creole is based, the language is said to be **decreolized,** and the overlapping varieties of the language form a **postcreole continuum** (see §11.6, *Hawaiian English*).

Jamaica was captured by the British in 1655 from the Spanish, who during the previous century had settled the island and exterminated the Arawak Indian population. Jamaican Pidgin English was the result of contact between these British settlers—many from the west of England, Ireland, and Scotland by way of Barbados, as well as from London—and the West Africans whom they imported as slaves to the sugar plantations. Because the slaves were brought from the Gold Coast, Nigeria, the Congo, and Angola, they were linguistically diverse, speaking languages in the Niger-Congo and West Sudanese families. Of these, Twi contributed the predominant share of loanwords, possibly because of the linguistic homogeneity of Gold Coast slaves and the early establishment of their leadership in Jamaica.[8]

The following passage is the beginning of a story in Jamaican Creole narrated by a man about 80 years old in the village of Accompong. It is given in conventional spelling along with a phonetic transcription of the creole pronunciation. In the old man's speech, [d] occurs instead of Standard English [ð], as in [dɑt] 'that'; [t] occurs instead of Standard English [θ], [tri] 'three'; [b] often occurs instead of Standard English [v], [juɔbiɑl] 'jovial'; the diphthongs [iɛ] in [niɛm] 'name', and [uɔ] in [uɔl] 'old' are rising diphthongs, with stress on the second element; and the diphthongs [ɑɪ] in [gwɑɪŋ] 'going', and [ɔʊ] in [nɔʊ] 'now' are falling diph-thongs, with stress on the first element. As in other creole languages, inflections are drastically reduced, with a correspondingly more rigid word order than in Standard English, and the copula is often omitted.

---

[7]Copyright "The Sunday Post." Reprinted by permission of the publishers, D. C. Thomson & Co. Ltd., Dundee, Scotland.

[8]For an excellent historical introduction to Jamaican Creole, see Le Page's chapters in R. B. Le Page and David DeCamp, *Jamaican Creole* (London: Macmillan, 1960).

Figure 10.1

William Saves His Sweetheart[9]

Now a old-time Anancying story we going at now. Now once there was a old witch-
nɔʊ, ʊɔl taɪm ɑnɑnsɪ-ɪn stuɔrɪ, wɛ gwaɪŋ at nɔʊ. nɔʊ wants dɛr   waz, a ʊɔl wɪč

lady live, had one son, name of William. William were engage to a young lady from a
liɛdɪ lɪv, had wan sʌn, niɛm av wɪljam. wɪljam wʌr ɪngiɛǰ, tu a jʌŋ   liɛdɪ, fram a

next old witch's section who was her mother-in law [stepmother]. Now that girl's
nɛks ʊɔl wɪč   sɛkšan hu   waz har madar ɪn la:.   nɔʊ dat gjʌl

father had that girl with his first wife. And after the wife decease, he is marry a next
fada, had dat gjʌl wɪd ɪz   fʌs waɪf. an afta   dɪ waɪf dɪsɪs,   hi ɪz marɪ a nɛks

woman, which is a old witch. And that woman bear two dauthers besides. Now the
wʊman wɪč   ɪs a ʊɔl wɪč. an   dat wʊman biɛr tu   da:taz. bɪsaɪdz. nɔʊ dɪ

three sisters living good [got along well together], but the mother-in-law didn't like that
tri   sɪstaz lɪvɪŋ gʊd,   bʌt dɪ mada ɪn la: dɪdn laɪk dat

one daughter at all, the man's. She prefer her own two. But yet the three girls were
wan da:ta   atal, fɪ-dɪ man. hɪm prɛfar fɪ-ar   tu.   bʌt, jɛt dɪ tri   gjʌl wər

jovial with one another. Well, that one girl was friends with this young man, name of
juɔbɪal wɪd wan ɑnada. wɛl, dat wan gjʌl,   frɛnz   wɪd dis jəŋ   man, niɛm av

William. William's mother is a old witch. The girl's mother-in-law is a old witch.
wɪljam. wɪljam   mada ɪz a uɔld wɪč. dɪ   gjʌl mada:nla: ɪz a uɔld wɪč.

So you going to find out what is going to happen now.
suɔ, ju gwaɪŋ   faɪn ɔʊt, wa dɛ gə   hapm nɔʊ.

English in Asia and Africa

To show the present diverse shape of the English language we should have dozens of examples, written and oral, from societies and classes around the world. In countries of Asia and Africa where English is widely spoken and written as a second language, the examples would form a spectrum, with pidgin at one extreme and the international variety of Standard English at the other. The selections below illustrate one variety only from several countries where English is an indispensable second language.

India

"Evils of Dowry System," letter to the editor, *The Hindu* (Madras), 18 July 1980.

Sir,—The prevalence of dowry is only one of the symptoms of the wide-spread national male-diction with ramifications in every field from Parliament to educational institutions. We see now a conspicuous deterioration of values in all faculties as the whole nation is oriented towards 'quick-

[9]Reprinted by permission of Macmillan Publishers, Ltd., from Le Page and DeCamp, *op. cit.,* p. 143. DeCamp's phonemic notation is adapted to the system of transcription used throughout this *Companion.*

money making' with less labour and least effort. Self-dignity and integrity of a person have become obsolete ethics to be scoffed at as they have become deterrents to the pace of amassing wealth and instantaneous prosperity. So even before this clamour to prosperity ends in vulgarity, let us rise up to revive our cherished values.

In this context, the parents and the marriageable children should first of all realise that marriage is above all a harmonious continuum of sharing of every phase of the (vicissitudes) of human experiences and so the married couple should be allowed to make their own independent life, earning their bread and winning mutual respect. The happiness of conjugal life is in struggling and seeking to fulfill the wishes and aspirations of the partners through adjustments and sacrifices in a give and take process. Borrowed wealth in the name of dowry is only surreptitious embezzlement and the monetary satiation out of it will wither away soon with the waning of this ill gotten wealth. For a youngman who takes the hand of a girl in marriage with sacred promises by holding her hand in one hand and demanding (or acquiesce to his parents' demand) and appropriating by the other hand an unscrupulous amount in cash and kind is total disgrace and dishonour. And it is equally degrading for the girl to be sold for a price losing her identity.

The substantial contributive factor towards the perpetuation of the demoralising system lies mainly with the hypocrisy of the 'parents' community. There is a section of the affluent and the "nouve riche" who are frantically clamouring to show off their wealth and pomp at all available opportunities and a family marriage happens to be the first and the best stage to give vent to their pride. Of late this malaise has also percolated to the middle class parents who in a bid to trumpet their so called status and power go all out to pay off huge sums for a groom irrespective of the suitability of the match. What counts for them is not their daughter's happiness and welfare but their own ego satisfaction. Umpteen cases are there where the parents go to the extent of selling their daughter to an unknown groom even agains the wishes of their daughter just to breed their pride.

Rather than perorate further, I will say that it is high time that committed groups of youngmen and women organised themselves not only to make vows to abolish dowry but take upon themselves the task of educating the public on the new values. The anger and indignation and the sense of outrage against dowry should be transferred into organised protest on the whole society.

Kenya

"Let People Speak Their Own Way," letter to the editor, *The Standard* (Nairobi), 11 April 1980.

Much has been written in your column about English spoken in our African countries.

What *wananchi* [citizens] should know is, we cannot in anyway stop "aping" whites, because we are trying to be as advanced as they are. If not, why do we go to school, churches and put on clothes that the whites brought?

However, although we are 'aping' whites, that does not force us to talk like them. We have our own African 'English' or even tribal 'English'.

For instance, there are some weakness in other tribes dialect, e.g. Some Luhya say Tse things are 'koot' meaning the things are good. The Luo will say 'No opposison' meaning 'No opposition' and Kikuyus will say 'I am alound' meaning I am around too etc.

So let people speak the way their tongues can allow provided words are written correctly.

Indonesia

"Robber Caught Red-Handed," news article, *The Indonesian Times* (Djakarta), 29 August 1980.

The police arrested one of two crafty felons who were caught red handed committing a robbery in the house of Miss Eeng, Villa Tanahmas, Jakarta Bypass, on Monday.

The would-be victim has been informed that she would be robbed by her friend, who by unbelievable coincidence happened to be a close friend of the aforementioned felons. Based on this information, she reported all of the details to the police.

Since they were aware of the planned robbery, the police had been lurking in front of Eeng's house since Monday morning. At a definite time, they saw two young men casing the joint on a trail motorcycle.

The police, however were not fully assured that the two motorcyclists were indeed the fellows for whom the intensive surveillance was intended, this was because they did not cruise up in a Corolla sedan as the information had suggested. The police however, were very on the ball and cleverly disconnected the sparkplug of the possible getaway machine.

After having been watched for 15 minutes, one of the crafty criminals confronted the police, who undertook routine questioning, he boldly claimed that he was the owner of the house. Surprisingly the police bit suspicious were not in the least and let him go. After half an hour, the other suspect was still in the house which caused the police to become somewhat suspicious of his intentions.

The police burst into the house and arrested a man after having caught him red hand with a deadly weapon and piles of loot. They also found that the house maid was securely tied up in her room.

During interrogation, the robber admitted to have just come from Australia a month ago. Since he was stoney broke, without a rupiah to his name, he was forced to commit the robbery, he said.

The police are still intensively searching for another robber, who managed to get clean away after having fooled them most effectively.

11

The English Language in America

11.1 QUESTIONS FOR REVIEW

1. Explain why the following people are important in historical discussions of the English language:

Noah Webster
Benjamin Franklin
James Russell Lowell
H. L. Mencken
Hans Kurath
Leonard Bloomfield
Noam Chomsky
William Labov

2. Define, identify, or explain briefly:

Old Northwest Territory
An American Dictionary of the English Language (1828)
The American Spelling Book
"Flat *a*"
African American Vernacular English
Pidgin
Creole
Gullah
Americanism
Linguistic Atlas of the United States and Canada
Phoneme
Allophone
Generative grammar

3. What three great periods of European immigration can be distinguished in the peopling of the United States?

4. What groups settled the Middle Atlantic States? How do the origins of these settlers contrast with the origins of the settlers in New England and the South Atlantic states?

5. What accounts for the high degree of uniformity of American English?

6. Is American English more or less conservative than British English? In trying to answer the question, what geographical divisions must one recognize in both the United

States and Britain? Does the answer that applies to pronunciation apply also to vocabulary?

7. What considerations moved Noah Webster to advocate a distinctly American form of English?

8. In what features of American pronunciation is it possible to find Webster's influence?

9. What are the most noticeable differences in pronunciation between British and American English?

10. What three main dialects in American English have been distinguished by dialectologists associated with the Linguistic Atlas of the United States and Canada? What three dialects had traditionally been distinguished?

11. According to Baugh and Cable, what eight American dialects are prominent enough to warrant individual characterization?

12. What is the **creole hypothesis** regarding African American Vernacular English?

13. To what may one attribute certain similarities between the speech of New England and that of the South?

14. To what may one attribute the preservation of *r* in American English?

15. To what extent are attitudes which were expressed in the nineteenth-century "controversy over Americanisms" still alive today? How pervasive now is the "purist attitude"?

16. What are the main historical dictionaries of American English?

11.2 THE AMERICAN DIALECTS (§250)

1. Each of the words below has regional variants of pronunciation that distinguish the major American dialects. Refer to Baugh and Cable §250 to fill in as much of the chart as you can with the relevant phonetic transcriptions, leaving blank the pronunciations in regions that are not discussed.

	Eastern New England	New York City	Upper North	Lower North	Upper South	Lower South	Your Pronunciation
hot							
fast							
car							
cot							
caught							
curl							
hoarse							
horse							
with							

	Eastern New England	New York City	Upper North	Lower North	Upper South	Lower South	Your Pronunciation
grease (v.)							
greasy							
roots							
forest							
care							
I							
out							
yes							
kept							
Tuesday							
pen							

2. What are the main features of General American? _____

_____

3. Which of the American dialects does your own speech most closely correspond to? In what features, if any, does it diverge from the dialect of the area where you live? _____

_____

_____

11.3 AFRICAN AMERICAN VERNACULAR ENGLISH: PHONOLOGY (§250)

Although most individual features of phonology and grammar that occur in African American Vernacular English occur also in other varieties of English at comparable socioeconomic levels, the features listed in this section and the next are significant for their particular array within AAVE.[1]

Description	Standard English	AAVE
1. Reduction of final consonant clusters	list [lɪst]	lis' [lɪs]
2. Plural formation that follows change 1 above	lists [lɪsts]	lisses [lɪsiz]

[1]The summaries and examples in this section and the next are drawn from various studies by William Labov, Bengt Loman, Walt Wolfram, Ralph W. Fasold, John Baugh, and John Rickford, including *African-American English: Structure, History and Use,* ed. Salikoko S. Mufwene, John R. Rickford, Guy Bailey, and John Baugh (Routledge: London, 1998).

Description	Standard English	AAVE
3. Loss of postvocalic liquids, [r] and [l]i	four [for]	fo' [fo]
4. Loss of postvocalic final stops and (less frequently) fricatives	boot [but]	boo' [bu]
5. Initial [d] for [ð]	the, they, that [ð]	de, dey, dat [d]
6. Initial [t] or [θ] for [θ]	thought [θ]	tough' [t] or though' [θ]
7. Medial [f] for [θ]	nothing [θ]	nuf'n [f]
8. Final [f] for [θ]	mouth [θ]	mouf [f]
9. [ɪn] for the -ing suffix [ɪŋ]	singing [sɪŋɪŋ]	singin' [sɪŋɪn]

Each of the following sentences contains words that illustrate features of AAVE pronunciation from the list above. Write down each word that illustrates a feature, and after it in parentheses give the number of the feature. For nonstandard pronunciations that are not described in the list, circle the words, taking care not to mark pronunciations that everyone uses.

1. Now what they be doin' that fo' I don't know.   *doin' (9), fo' (3)*

2. One day, I was, I was jus' sleepin'.

3. I'm tellin' ne truf abou' i'. I don' have one.

4. So then tha' thing got turned out, an' I was tryin' to fin' my cousin Ruth.

5. So, Verne was gonna go wif us.

6. I tink some'm goin' on out dere.

7. We have geography tes' one day. Den we ha' spellin tes' one day.

8. We have tes'es jus' bou' everyday bu' we don' have homework jus' bou' everyday. __

_____

_____

9. It won't be nofin' to do till he fin' out can he go wifout takin' John. _____

_____

_____

10. She don' wan' nobody in her house so she a'ways comin' in our house. _____

_____

_____

11.4 AFRICAN AMERICAN VERNACULAR ENGLISH: GRAMMAR (§250)

Some features of AAVE that appear to be grammatical are actually phonological, a result of the regular application of principles of pronunciation such as those described in the preceding section rather than principles of morphology. *Pass,* for example, could be the past tense form that results from a simplification of consonants in *passed* [pæst] and not the product of a nonstandard grammatical paradigm that specifies no ending. Phonological variables obviously affect the grammatical paradigm, and the distinction between the two is sometimes hard to draw. The following features can with good reason be considered *grammatical* features of AAVE.

1. Omission of the *-s* possessive suffix.
So you got *teacher* pencil in your pocket.
2. *Mines* for *mine.*
I ma tell my mother dat you trow *mines* up dere on ne roof.
3. *Ain't* for *didn't* in negation.
I *ain'*ha' my play clothes on.
4. Double negative (negative concord).
You *ain'* got *no* cash money.
5. Absence of *be* in structures containing:

  a. Predicate adjective
    He crazy anyway.
  b. Predicate nominative
    She a nurse.
  c. Predicate phrase of place or time
    We on tape.
  d. Verb + *-ing.*
    He just fell like he gettin' cripple up from arthritis.

6. Invariant *be* in structures containing[2]

    a. Predicate adjective
      They sometimes *be* incomplete and things like that.

    b. Predicate nominative
      He sometimes *be* a operator doctor.

    c. Predicate phrase of place or time
      That's why I wonder why I don't see him—he usually be round.

    d. Verb + *-ing*
      Well, sometime she *be* fighting in school and out on the playground.

7. *I'm gonna* reduced to *I mana, I mon,* or *I ma.*
    I ma tell you another story about a . . . white man.

8. Stressed *been* to indicate action or state in the remote past.
    She *BEEN* married. [She been married for a long time (and still is).]

9. Use of *done* to emphasize the completed nature of an action.
    He *done* did it.

10. Absence of subject relative pronoun.
    That's the man come here. [That's the man who came here.]

Indicate the grammatical features of AAVE that are illustrated in the sentences by supplying numbers that refer to the list above. Then write the Standard English version of each nonstandard sentence.

    1. She ain't tell me that today, you know. She BEEN tell me that. _____*3, 8*_____ *She didn't tell me that today, you know. She told me that a long time ago.*

_____

    2. That Shirley, she so worried, she just don't want to be with nobody. _____

_____

_____

    3. I be on the telephone and he be going, "Where you went today?" _____

_____

_____

    4. And then he said, "I'ma bring my people." _____

_____

_____

    5. He the man got all the old records. _____

_____

_____

---

[2]The invariant *be* that results from phonological processes—specifically the contraction of will be *(He be here pretty soon)*—should be distinguished from grammatically invariant *be (Sometime he be there and sometime he don't).* The latter structure has been described as marking a grammatical category of "habitual" or "durative" in AAVE: "[A] semantic analysis of the marker *be*...shows that the AAVE system has a way of marking habituality which is not available in SAE [Standard American English]." (Lisa Green, "Aspect and Predicate Phrases in African-American Vernacular English," in Mufwene et al., p. 45.) A similar usage has been observed in Anglo-Irish.

6. My hair BEEN cut._____

_____

_____

7. When they used to tell us that the nipples be pink on pregnant women, we be laughin'. _____

_____

8. If I go in Miss Barbara house she gon be tryin' to make me get ou'. _____

_____

_____

9. Look! I done cooked a turkey! _____

_____

_____

10. You out the game. _____

_____

_____

11. Hey baby, this be Heywood!_____

_____

_____

12. It ain't no way no girl can't wear no platforms to no amusement park. _____

_____

_____

11.5 PRESENT DIFFERENTIATION OF VOCABULARY (§253)

Match the numbers of the things in the picture with the British English words below. Give the corresponding words in American English:

accumulator, bathing costume, bonnet, boot, braces, call box, caravan, carriage dustbin, engine-driver, estate car, flyover, letter box, lorry, motorway, numberplate, plimsolls, roof rack, rowing boat, sailing boat, silencer, sleeper, spanner, windscreen

British English	*American English*
1. _____	_____
2. _____	_____
3. _____	_____

Figure 11.1

4. _____

5. _____

6. _____

7. _____

8. _____

9. _____

10. _____

11. _____

12. _____

13. _____

14. _____

15. _____

16. _____

17. _____

18. _____

19. _____

20. _____

21. _____

22. _____

23. _____

24. _____

11.6 *DICTIONARY OF AMERICAN REGIONAL ENGLISH, DARE* (§255)

Although proposals for a dictionary of American regional English had been made since the founding of the American Dialect Society in 1889, it was not until 1962 that the project became fully organized and substantially funded under the editorship of Frederic G. Cassidy. Three of the four volumes have now been published.[3] The main corpus of data was gathered by eighty-two fieldworkers, chiefly graduate students in English language and linguistics, but also some undergraduates and college teachers. Between 1965 and 1970 the fieldworkers conducted interviews of 2777 informants in 1002 communities throughout the United States. The computer-generated maps that accompany some of the items are populational, not areal. In drawing the size of each state to reflect its population, this format adjusts and distorts the familiar shapes

---

[3]*Dictionary of American Regional English,* ed. Frederic G. Cassidy, 3 vols. of 4 in press (Cambridge, MA: Harvard UP, 1985, 1991, 1996). Map reprinted by permission of Harvard University Press.

of the states accordingly. Thus, the 1002 communities are represented as evenly distributed on the population map:

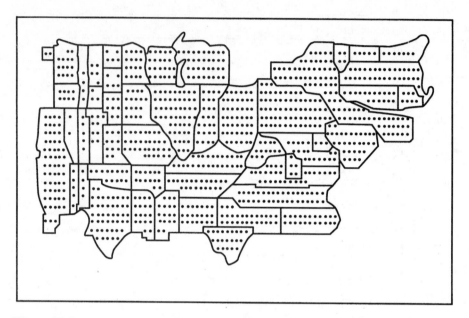

Figure 11.2

Many words recorded in *DARE* have a clearly limited regional distribution, occurring rarely or not at all in other regions. For each word below give the region where it mainly occurs, as reported in *DARE*. For those words that you are not familiar with, give also the definition. Some words have fairly obvious historical, cultural, climatic, or other geographical reasons for their distribution. Note down any explanations for these distributions that occur to you or that you can infer from the citations.

armoire _____

_____

_____

arroyo _____

_____

_____

baga _____

_____

_____

bear claw _____

_____

_____

bismarck _____

_____

_____

blue norther _____

_____

_____

bobsleigh _____

_____

_____

buttery _____

_____

_____

buttonwood _____

_____

_____

carry (sense 1) _____

_____

_____

clapboard (noun) _____

_____

_____

clearseed _____

_____

_____

down cellar _____

_____

_____

Dutch cheese _____

_____

_____

evening _____

_____

_____

fastnacht _____

_____

_____

flannel cake _____

_____

_____

fox and geese (sense 2) _____

_____

_____

freeway _____

_____

frijole_____

_____

frontage road _____

_____

greasy (form 1). Pronunciation: _____

_____

greasy (form 2). Pronunciation: _____

_____

_____

hero _____

_____

_____

11.7 THE LANGUAGE ILLUSTRATED (§250)

Appalachian English

Within the extensive range of the Appalachian Mountains, the area most typically referred to as Appalachia includes parts of Kentucky, Virginia, North Carolina, and Tennessee and all of West Virginia. The variety of American English spoken in this mountainous area west of the

Virginia Piedmont and north of the Plantation South is known as Upper South, South Midland, or Mid-Southern. (See the map in Baugh and Cable, p. 377.) The following example is an excerpt from an interview with a 67-year-old retired miner, a resident of the southern part of West Virginia.[4]

> Oh, that's outrageous and not only that, whiskey. Whiskey should be outlawed, all kind of dope. It's just like putting a dang hog in a corn crib full of corn and say "Don't eat that corn!" Well now, that pig's gonna eat some of that corn. Same way with this other junk a-running around over the country. That dope, you know people has to try and be seen. Like, the man from Missouri, he don't believe it, he got to show him. So, all these, not all, but a lot of these teenagers, "Let me try that!" And, if they get a kick out of it, it's like taking a drink of whiskey, you take a drink or two of whiskey and it makes you feel pretty good, you want another 'n, you want to feel better. And the more you drink the better you feel 'til I reckon you feel, the first thing you know, you don't know anything. You're dead to the world. And then, a lot of 'em go on and drink every day, after they get into it and that puts 'em on the green hillside. Oh, I'll tell you, I read a little article in a paper, in a magazine, where some dude said, yesterday would make, I mean, the girls of today woulda made mothers of yesterday ashamed of theirself cooking. That the girls this day and time cook so much better. If they couldn't get it out of a tin can they couldn't cook you a can of soup. It comes out of the can and bread offa' the shelf. Well, that's ruined more good women than anything in the world this old light bread. My old woman in there has made as good a biscuits than you ever stuck in your mouth, but she's got away from it, and she don't make 'em often enough. I don't care what you do, you got to keep it up in order to do it good and properly.

African American Vernacular English

The speaker in the following passage is a young African American woman from South Central Los Angeles, the area that includes Watts. She recounts an incident of ghetto life to a white female researcher.[5] Refer to §§11.4 and 11.5 for phonological and syntactic features of African American Vernacular English.

> My close friends, who are they? I have a lotta *associates* but you really don' know who you friends are until you git into a bind. Den you know who comes to your rescue. Now I got one person, I can really say is my friend. She just like family.
>
> I got cut over my baby's father. I was cut, I thought it was jus' a little thing. Beverly seen my dress covered wi' blood. She say, "Girl, you goin' to d' hospital." "I ain't goin' to no hospital! I ain' cut dat bad!" She say, "Lemme see." So she raised down d' back o' my dress and she looked at it and she say, "Girl, you settin' *wide* open! You gonna go to d' hospital if I gotta drag you!"
>
> I was bleedin' so bad, 'cause every time I close my neck back, it would close it. So, she had d' window up and I could see myself passin' out and she kep' on constantly talkin' to me, so I wouldn't pass out.
>
> When dey got me to the hospital and put me on d' stretcher, she seen me and I was dozin' off. Everytime I *try* to doze off, she come an' wake me, she gimme cigarettes, she did everything to keep me awake—which she did—until they stitch me up. Had fourteen stitches. Now Beverley, she a righteous hope-to-die partner!

---

[4]Reprinted by permission of the Center for Applied Linguistics, from Walt Wolfram and Donna Christian, *Appalachian Speech* (Arlington, Va.: Center for Applied Linguistics, 1976), p. 176.

[5]Reprinted by permission of Harvard University Press, from Edith A. Folb, *Runnin' Down Some Lines: The Language and Culture of Black Teenagers* (Cambridge, Mass.: Harvard University Press, 1980), p. 25.

Hawaiian English

The English language in Hawaii more than anywhere else in the United States challenges the linguist to rethink and make precise such terms as *pidgin, creole,* and *dialect.* The insights that are gained from examining the extreme varieties of Hawaiian English have obvious applications in understanding the more muted differences on the mainland between African American Vernacular English and Standard English.

Captain Cook and his men first brought English to the Hawaiian Islands in 1778. They were followed by fur and sandalwood traders during the next half century and by whalers after 1829. Although British English was the variety of the language first heard in Hawaii, the arrival of New England missionaries in 1820 established the American variety, which became increasingly prominent during the latter part of the nineteenth century. An English-Hawaiian pidgin developed, characterized by the reduced structure and vocabulary of pidgin languages. As later generations learned the pidgin as a native language and reexpanded its structure and vocabulary, it became creolized. The English creole in Hawaii was enriched by the Chinese and Portuguese languages spoken by laborers who came to the sugar plantations during the 1870s and 1880s, and later by the languages of the Japanese, the Koreans, the Filipinos, and the Puerto Ricans.

The distinction between Hawaiian Pidgin English and Hawaiian Creole English is fairly clear, a pidgin historically having no native speakers. The distinction between Hawaiian Creole English and Hawaiian dialects of English is more problematical, since dialects of English can vary far from Standard English without being creoles. Sociolinguists have proposed a system of overlapping varieties in Hawaiian English, from Creole at one extreme to Standard English at the other, a system that may be represented as overlapping circles.[6]

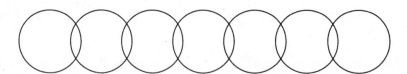

Figure 11.3

If we designate the leftmost circle as the English-based creole (or **basilect**) and the rightmost circle as Standard English, we can speak of a **postcreole continuum.** The overlapping intermediate circles represent various stages of decreolization, called **mesolects.** The two versions of the Prodigal Son that follow are located at different places on the continuum. The first one, which has some inauthentic features and exaggeration for comic effect but which is a fairly accurate representation, would fall nearer the right end of the spectrum. The second, which has been described as "almost authentic enough to qualify as source material,"[7] would fall nearer the left end. Some of the words in it would have been used only by elderly Japanese of the period.

[6]See Richard R. Day, "Decreolization: Coexistent Systems and the Post-Creole Continuum," in *Pidgins and Creoles: Current Trends and Prospects,* ed. David DeCamp and Ian F. Hancock (Washington, D.C.: Georgetown University Press, 1974), p. 39.

[7]John E. Reinecke et al., *A Bibliography of Pidgin and Creole Languages* (Honolulu: University Press of Hawaii, 1975), p. 594.

Characteristic features of Hawaiian English that show up in one or both of the passages are the alternation between [d] and [ð] in words like *this (dis);* the alternation between [t] and [θ] in words like *thing (everything);* an *r* pronunciation for Standard English [l]; the occurrence of Hawaiian loanwords (*luau* 'party', 'feast'; *hana hana* 'work', 'activity'; *aikane* 'friend'; *aloha* 'love', 'affection', 'hello', 'goodbye') and of loanwords from other languages (*kaukau* 'food', 'eat', probably an adaptation of Cantonese Pidgin English *chow-chow*). Syntactic features that commonly occur also in other creole languages are copula deletion *(he poor man);* the use of preposed particles for negation *(no make luau);* and the use of single, uninflected verbs for verb phrases *(today he come home).*

"Evangelist Speak, Prodigal Son Get Too Muchee Nice Kind Luau" in the *Honolulu Star-Bulletin* about 1929.[8]

> One time one old man he got two son, speak inside Bible. . . . One old son and one young son. This young son he too much pakiki [headstrong]. He speak the old man, "Give me my share—I like go nother prace. I tired dis prace."
> So papa he give his share and the old brother his share—all same half half.
> Pretty soon bimeby young son he go nother prace look see. He trow away everythings he got. He lose all money. He make big luau [party], he drink plenty okolehao [native brew], shoots crap, play card, anykine he do. He find plenty wahine [women] make big time—all same haole speak hoopee.
> Dar arri, bimeby money all pau [gone, finished]. Ikane [*aikane,* friends] pau. Kaukau [food] pau. Everyting pau. He look see jobs but no kind find. Erri prace he go—speak me too sorry dis time, country got dispression dis time, no home hanahana [work] gotch.
> He speak, "Auwe [alas], wasamatta for me dis time too much pilikia [trouble]." Porice speak no stop dis prace. Erribody speak dis fella no more good. Auwe for dis fella dis time no more luau. He eat any kine kaukau—puaa [hog, pig] kaukau [food] he kaukau [eat]!
> Bimeby dis fella he tink plenty man work my father prace. Papa he got all kine good kaukau, more betta I go home stop. Spose old man he huhu [gets angry with] me I speak him nice ting. Me speak I too much sorry. Maybe bimeby erriting more betta.
> He go home. Father he look see his son all time—he too much like dis boy—bimeby he look see son he come. He run outside quick for see boy. He speak, "Aroha, me too much grad you come, rong time no see."
> Father he too much grad. He tell man bring new crothes, new shoes, gold ring—anykine he give dis boy.
> Bimbey papa he tell cook make big luau—kill puaa kill pipi kane [figuratively speaking, the fatted calf], plenty kine kaukau he tell him fix.
> He tell erribody come eat. Play music, dance hula—plenty good time.
> Big brother he too much huhu [angry]. He speak father, "Wasamatta you. I stay home hanahana. No drink okolehao, no make luau, nobody make good time for me."
> Father tell him, "Wasamatta you wassamatta me—you wassamatta! Dis boy he bad boy. He go nother prace make haole kine hoopee. He spend all money bimby he broke he come home. He speak he too much sorry. I grad to see dis boy—long time no see. He is prodigal son. We make big luau."

From the *Honolulu Advisor,* 11 May 1924, reprinted in William C. Smith, "Pidgin English in Hawaii," *American Speech,* 8 (1933), 16. This portion begins with the celebration at the return of the "number two boy."

[8]Reprinted with glosses in John E. Reinecke, *Language and Dialect in Hawaii: A Sociolinguistic History to 1935,* ed. S. M. Tsuzaki (Honolulu: University Press of Hawaii, 1969), pp. 218–19. Reprinted by permission of the *Honolulu Star-Bulletin.*

Bime by all men utauta no, all men yo-ro-di-bu. Bime by number one boy, he nother
By an by   *sing*   *happy*

place hana hana. He come home time, he too muchee utauta kiku. He cook men tou:
         work   *singing hear.*   *ask*

"All men nani inside hana hana." Cook man speakee: "Number two muskee, you nisan,
          what   *activity*   *brother*

long time nother place go; today he come home. Papa speakee luau hana hana, all men
                                                                 feast

guru kaukau tabelu, utauta hana hana no." Ah ya, number one boy, ah ray, this time
         food   *sing*

sabe, inside lili huhu no. He papa like talk talk. Papa come. Number one musko talkee,
understand   *little angry*

talkee: "Wassamala you this number two brudder to muchee luau hana hana.
         What's the matter with

Number two brudder, ah ray, he house no stop long time. You dale makana he nother
                                       stay   *dollars give*

place go; dala all spendo. He poor man. He dala no more; he wiki-wiki papa house
                                                                    hurry

come home. He come home time you luau hana hana. Wassamala   me long time
                                       feast   *What's the matter*

you house stop, you me no more luau you hana hana, guru clothes you no makana; me
      stay   *give*

aikane no more con doh, mamona ushi no hana make, me kaukau doh. Wasamala, papa
friends   *fat*   *calf*   *kill*   *food*

you me no more aloha no!" "Ah ya," papa talk, "you brudder long time he go, me
                love

thinkee make no but today he come home no. Me too muchee aloha number two
         dead   *love*

brudder, all same you too, aloha pololei, number two brudder, you, me, all same aloha."
                                   right